POLAND

U

VAKIA

pest
RY

ROMANIA

Bucharest

Belgrade

LIA

Sofia

ALBANIA

GREECE

Athens

Black Sea

Ankara

TURKEY

Cyprus

Crete

ean Sea

Acre
Haifa
Jericho
PALESTINE
Jaffa
Jerusalem

Derna

Tobruk

Barce

Benghazi

Bardia
Sidi Barrani

Mersah Matruh
Maaten Bagush
El Daba

Sollum

Buq Buq

Alexandria

Sidi Omar

El Alamein

Suez

Qattara
Depression

Cairo

A

Siwa

EGYPT

MY
FATHER'S SON

MY
FATHER'S SON

THE MEMOIRS OF

MAJOR THE EARL HAIG

OBE DL ARSA

LEO COOPER

First published in Great Britain in 2000 by
LEO COOPER
an imprint of
Pen & Sword Books Ltd
47 Church Street
Barnsley
South Yorkshire
S70 2AS

A CIP record for this book is
available from the British Library

ISBN 0 85052 708 2

Typeset in Garamond 3 by
Phoenix Typesetting, Ilkley, West Yorkshire

Printed in England by
Redwood Books Ltd, Trowbridge, Wilts.

Dedication

This book is dedicated to Queen Elizabeth the Queen Mother, in tribute to her steadfast guidance over the years, and to her Majesty's ability to impart strength and sympathy to all those who have had the honour of speaking to her.

Contents

Acknowledgements

First of all I offer my thanks to the late Miss I. G. Campbell, MBE, who typed the original draft over thirty years ago. Having rewritten the text, I have been lucky this past year to have my present secretary, Mrs Gavin Tweedie, to retype it and help with the index. My wife, Fruzzy, has encouraged me to produce something worthy of the scrutiny of Brigadier Henry Wilson, Publishing Director of Pen & Sword. Tom Hartman, the publisher's editor and a former 11th Hussar, has given me helpful advice over the script and the photographs.

I am grateful to the late Sir Hugh Brassey, through his widow Joyce, to John Warrender, now Lord Bruntisfield, and to Colonel Aidan Sprot for giving us an insight into the lighter side of regimental life in the Middle East.

My thanks are also due to the Duke of Buccleuch for letting me publish a letter of condolence from his father, a good friend in sunshine and in shadow. I should also mention my mother's contributions which express her liveliness in the days before she had to conform to the responsibilities of a senior officer's wife and to work in helping men disabled in the First World War.

I must also thank Mrs Victor Pasmore and Lady Gowing for allowing me to include interesting letters about my time at the Camberwell School of Art. Lord Halifax has allowed me to publish his uncle Peter Wood's poem about Oxford and

Derek Hill to include his encouraging words written at an early stage in my artistic career. I am grateful to Mrs Michael Riviere for allowing me to quote her late husband's 'Colditz' poem and to Mat Tunnock who made excellent copies of a number of the photographs used in the book.

Contributions from my late sisters Xandra and Doria have helped to describe my father.

Preface

In this book I offer some reminiscences of the first thirty years of my life. They were put down when I had suffered a riding accident which incapacitated me, so writing helped to pass the time. Now it is time to present that manuscript in a form which I hope readers of my own and of younger generations will find enjoyable and of some interest.

Although my father died when I was only nine, I have memories of a warm family life which were very happy thanks to him and to the atmosphere which he created. As I wrote in my foreword to *The Private Papers of Douglas Haig*, edited by Robert Blake, "Perhaps our family crest, the rock, is symbolic of my father's character: but to picture him as a hard, unfeeling man is wrong". His death shattered the solidity of our home background, but, thanks to good friends and relations, my younger sister Irene and I survived to tell the tale. My mother, in spite of ill health, worked in devotion to my father's memory for ex-servicemen until her death in 1939.

My heritage at an early age was in some ways presented on a silver spoon in that I was able to enjoy the Border country-side and country pursuits, but was marred by financial difficulties and the responsibilities of succeeding a great man whose duties reflected his greatness.

I was lucky to enjoy considerable happiness at school, particularly at my public school, Stowe, where I was free to roam the country, keep dogs and, latterly, a horse. These addictions, which were part of my father's traditions in the cavalry, continued during my three years at Oxford.

When the war came I was able to sidestep military training at Sandhurst, having qualified for a Regular Commission by means of a University degree and service in the OTC, and joined a Scottish regiment, the Royal Scots Greys. Service in Palestine and the Western Desert resulted in my being taken prisoner during the first Battle of Alamein in July 1942.

That experience had a profound effect on me. I was suffering from amoebic dysentery when I was captured, so that to maintain morale was a challenge. My earlier background of a life among "the gentry" was jolted into an awareness of the existence of the middle and working classes, which was salutary and which led to the widening of my mental frontiers and to a more meaningful life after the war.

During my captivity I developed a talent for painting which I practised by making portraits of my fellow prisoners. So after the war I went for a while to a London art school – the Camberwell School of Arts and Crafts – where I was lucky to be taught by the founders of the Euston Road School, Coldstream, Pasmore and Rogers, and by Laurence Gowing. My early struggles to become a practising painter are described in this book.

One episode in my time as a POW which may be of special interest was when I became a Prominente at Colditz. A few relations of "important" figures in the British establishment had been selected by Hitler to be specially guarded. Ultimately we would probably have been used as hostages. It is perhaps doubtful whether our lives would have helped Hitler to save his skin, and during the last days in the Bunker he is said, according to my brother-in-law Hugh Trevor Roper in his book *The Last Days of Hitler*, to have ordered us to be shot. Certainly this caused us to endure much fear and anxiety, but in the end there was a happy outcome.

This short account describes the happenings of someone

who was already affected by a difficult childhood and up-
bringing when caught by the enemy and shut up in captivity.
It describes the effects of captivity on different kinds of
people and in some cases, myself included, where talents were
developed and benefit occurred. We came out different from
what we were before we went in. It was interesting to me to
be able to reflect, at the time I wrote the book, on some of
these changes.

As the painter Paul Klee put it in the Bauhaus Prospectus
in 1929, "One learns to look behind the facade to grasp the
root of things. One learns to recognize the undercurrents,
the antecedents of the visible. One learns to dig down, to
uncover, to find the cause, to analyse."

Oflag Night Piece

The poor man's wealth, the prisoner's release – Sir Philip Sidney

There, where the swifts flicker along the wall
And the last light catches, there in the high schloss
(How the town grows dark) all's made impregnable:
They bless each window with a double cross
Of iron; weave close banks of wire and train
Machine guns down on them; and look – at the first star
Floodlight the startled darkness back again . . .
All for three hundred prisoners of war.
Yet now past them and the watch they keep,
Unheard, invisible, in ones and pairs,
In groups, in companies – alarms are dumb,
A sentry loiters, a blind searchlight stares –
Unchallenged as their memories of home
The vanishing prisoners escape to sleep.

Michael Riviere,
Selected Poems
Mandeville Press, 1984

I

My Parents

My father, Douglas, was the youngest of the eleven children born to John Haig and his wife, Rachel Veitch. Of his brothers the third son died young and the fifth brother, George, died prematurely from eating bad watercress en route to Ireland and was taken off the Irish mail at Chester. His birth took place in Edinburgh in 1861 and his early life was spent at Cameron House in Fife. From the beginning his only form of transportation was on the back of a pony by means of a pannier or the saddle, and from an early age he and his brothers Bee and George rode their ponies, two of which were called "Bismarck" and "The General", across the flat open fields beside the Firth of Forth. My father was the Benjamin and perhaps the best-looking of the family, with long fair curls, a broad domed forehead and clear blue eyes. He was secure in the deep love given to him by his mother, which gave him a strength which would stand him in good stead throughout his life. He was at times wilful and difficult to manage, being cross and quick tempered. Due to the fact that he was his mother's favourite there were occasions when his elder brothers and sisters were overcome with resentment. One day they seized him, cut off his curls and ordered him to carry them in his pinafore to his mother, who with sadness put them carefully in a parcel. Thanks to her care they are preserved to this day.

Through this close relationship with his mother, who was

a deeply religious woman, though not a believer in the occult as were several of her children, my father was given a careful grounding in religion. Her mother, Philadelphia, had been the daughter of a Mr Robertson, the Minister of Norham. She heard the children's prayers night and morning, and every morning in winter and summer she got up about 4 am to see that all was well in the nursery. When she died at the early age of fifty-eight in 1879 my father was heartbroken. During the last days of her illness her son spent day after day during his holidays sitting by her bedside talking to her.

Douglas's father was a distiller, whose father had been a distiller before him. Our line descended from Robert Haig, the second son of the 17th Laird of Bemersyde, who had moved to St Ninians near Stirling in the 17th century. My great-grandfather, William Haig of Seggie, was Provost of St Andrews and a distiller, and had married his cousin Janet Stein of Kennetpans, the daughter of another distiller. Janet's mother Margaret had a dream in which her mother's ghost appeared to her and prophesied the future greatness of some member of the family. After that every Haig mother was hoping it would be her son.

William Haig had a kindly face, whereas his son John, my grandfather, had an austere look. In his will he stipulated that all his men could drink as much as they wanted on the day of his funeral. Perhaps understandably, there have been attempts to extend the terms of that will down to recent times. The turnout for his funeral was large and stretched the whole length of St Andrews.

In due course my father went to Oxford and in 1883 to Sandhurst where he won the Sword of Honour. One of the Instructors, on being asked who was the most promising cadet, replied, "A Scottish lad, Douglas Haig is top in everything, books, drill, riding and sports. He is to go into the cavalry and before he has finished he will be top of the Army."

In the Army my father became a dedicated professional

soldier at a time when the majority of his fellow officers found it easier to take life light-heartedly. His years of apprenticeship were spent with the 7th Hussars in India where he was described by his Troop Sergeant, Sergeant S. Griffiths:

"During that time Lieut. Haig was appointed Adjutant of the Regiment in succession to Captain Ridley – a great responsibility for an officer with so little service, but the Lieut. was equal to the work he had to do which was done in first class military style. . . . He would come down to hospital and talk to the serious cases, ask if he could do anything for you, he would write to your friends in England if you were not well enough . . . He was most kind to me."

During his time in India my father applied himself to soldiering with such seriousness that he can have had little time for the cultivation of outside interests. Through his dedication he sought the experience which would train him for higher command, a goal which he sought not so much for reasons of ambition but because of the sense of duty which was a key factor in his makeup. From India he returned to the Staff College. As a Staff Officer he served in the Sudan and later in South Africa. It is perhaps surprising that in 1905, at the late age of 44 as a Major General and Inspector General of Cavalry in India, whilst home on leave he decided to marry a young woman with a very different background to his own.

He was handsome, not tall, with a fine brow and a strong jaw which suggested a determined side to his personality. Beneath the good looks and the military appearance there lurked a depth of feeling which expressed itself through his sometimes twinkling, sometimes sad eyes, grey-blue in colour. He thought much and spoke little, with a slight hesitation which stemmed from shyness.

My mother was twenty years younger than he was. She had watched two years earlier, when she had been in attendance upon Queen Alexandra, my father playing in the final of the Inter-Regimental Polo Tournament at Hurlingham. My father had been captain of the 17th Lancers team in its victory over The Blues, and his bearing had made a deep impression on her. She had asked her brother George, a member of the Regiment, to introduce her after the match, but without success since her brother thought that my father had the reputation of being a woman hater.

My mother's family came from Glynn in Cornwall. Her father had served as Minister in Brussels and in Rome. Her great-grandfather, the first Lord Vivian, had commanded a cavalry brigade at Waterloo and had become Master General of the Ordnance. Her mother, a Miss Duff from Aberdeenshire, made beautiful needlework and tapestries which were used for firescreens and chairs, which are to be found in several family homes today. My father maintained that she arranged books according to their bindings rather than their contents after she had rearranged his library during one of his many moves. She was an enthusiastic gambler and eventually died at Monte Carlo, where she was cremated and was then transported in a casket by my uncle George to be reunited with my grandfather in the British cemetery in Rome. In spite of her elegance and imposing appearance, she was not alarming and she was a most warm and loving grandmother. I well remember her walking under the rookery at Bemersyde hoping that some bird droppings might fall on her hat and so bring her luck over her bets of the day. She was much younger than my Haig grandmother who died in 1878. She and her three daughters, my mother, Violet Vivian and Alexandra Worsley, and her son George were to play a considerable part in my childhood. Even so, Granny Vivian was quite old when I was born and my mother was old enough to have been my grandmother.

My mother and her twin sister Violet spent their childhood in the Embassies of Brussels and Rome. My mother always liked to remind us that she came second into the world, and as no preparations had been made for her arrival she spent her first few days in a drawer rather than in the family cot. Aunt Violet not only had the privilege of being the first born, she also had the good looks, the character and the charm which remained with her till the end of her days. My grandfather noticed my mother's lack of confidence and did his utmost to help her to overcome the inferiority complex from which she suffered. He was anxious that his daughters should learn to have independence, a rare quality in those days, and he would insist when they were quite young that they sometimes did up their own hair before dinner. Whenever they suffered from minor ailments he would go and see them and often administered the medicines himself.

Life in the Embassy must have been warm, civilized and cultivated judging by the signatures in my mother's album. Numbers of writers, painters and musicians came to stay there during their visits to Rome; Busoni, Augustus Hare and Alfred Tennyson were among those who drew and wrote poems for her. The twins were popular members of Roman society and they made many friends. My mother described her home life in those early days:

"I can recollect being very ill with the 'flu and quite delirious and hearing my father's kind voice through the wild fancies running through my head, feeling all was well that he was near. My mother was considered a very beautiful woman and wonderfully good at entertaining . . . and what beautiful surroundings the Embassy was in, on the old walls of Rome by the Porta Pia where Garibaldi entered Rome. The gardens on the walls were a mass of flowers and there were small lizards scrambling about."

The twins had different makeups, so it must have been hard for them to keep in step, wear the same dresses and do all the things which twins are expected to do. Their brother George described them in a poem he wrote on 7 February 1899:

A pair of twins there were whose looks
    So very different were;
One thought of dresses, Earls and dooks
    and also of her hair.

The other had a simpler taste,
    Untidiness was rife;
She cared not for the "Lotion Paste"
    Which some say makes a wife.

A sage then said with air divine,
    How better far 'twould be
Each other's thoughts to intertwine
    A medium thus we'd see.

My mother's harum-scarum nature was part of her attraction for my father. His priorities were illustrated in one of his favourite maxims: "What I most prize in a woman is her affection, not her intellect".

Sadly my grandfather died relatively young of cancer. Just before his death he had been appointed by the Queen as Ambassador in Paris. The Queen, in recognition of my grandfather's services to the country, decided to appoint one of his daughters as Maid of Honour. The choice had to be made between my mother and Aunt Violet. My mother described what happened:

"We had recently come to England after my father's death, and the Queen sent for us to come to Osborne to be 'looked at'. The Empress Frederick was staying there at the time, and her daughter had recently had twins. We were, therefore, for that reason of some interest. The Empress, who was standing behind the Queen's chair, asked us the difference in our age.

My sister who was always more forthcoming than I and who up to present had answered all the questions put to us said that she was a day older. But I could not stand this, and burst out with the remark 'only five minutes'. The Queen smiled and nodded her head. It was due to this remark I learnt afterwards that I was the one to be selected."

Queen Victoria probably fell for the greater liveliness of my mother, a quality which she much needed in the intimate circle of her court during the last sad years of her life. The Queen took great care of her Maids of Honour, supervising the preparation of their rooms herself. The Queen's kindness and warmth meant much to my mother. The Royal Household often had to appear in full or half mourning. During a half-mourning phase my mother ventured into mauve, but when one of the ladies went even further across the spectrum to a dusky shade of pink, all the ladies were ordered to restrict themselves to wearing grey. My mother described how, with the aid of a present of £100 from her uncle Charlie Duff Assheton Smith to supplement her meagre allowance, she was able to furnish her initial wardrobe:

"Oh, I enjoyed that shopping, and thinking myself so rich. Many may not have liked choosing so much black – but all was so new to me – and I revelled in the black gloves – black satin and duller black for deep mourning dresses and the sudden relief in mauve. I chose mauve because it was my favourite colour. And the shoes too, it was fun to swagger about and get them for the first time made for one. I had lovely paste buckles to each and trees each, and as can well be imagined, suddenly such a lot of money to spend only on oneself. I had got rid of the lot in a very short time!"

Matrimony also was frowned upon, particularly after one or two of the Maids of Honour left to get married, one of them to the court doctor sometime after the Queen had spied the couple among the shrubs as she drove past in her carriage. For some moments the Queen's concentration was lifted from the words being read to her by the Maid of Honour long enough for her to spot her enamoured medical practitioner through several pairs of glasses. My mother described the reading sessions:

> "We had received orders from the doctor that we were to see that Her Majesty was wrapped up warmly because the Queen always drove in an open carriage winter and summer and that we should keep her awake by reading to her. This reading in the carriage was often very difficult because the Queen usually chose the leading article of *The Times*, and when at Windsor especially, we had to drive over very bumpy ground. Very often the Queen would go off into a doze and we would lose our place. But unfortunately the Queen would remember where we had got to, and so I had to keep my finger on the spot so as to begin again where I had left off."

When my mother visited Her Majesty shortly before her death, she was asked by members of the Court to say how well she thought the Queen was looking. This she did, but the Queen replied that her end was not far away.

After the death of Queen Victoria my mother and Aunt Violet were appointed as two of the complement of six Maids of Honour to which Queen Alexandra as Queen Consort was entitled. Both my mother and Aunt Violet became devoted to the new Queen, a devotion which lasted throughout Queen Alexandra's life. Aunt Violet remained a Lady in Waiting to Queen Alexandra for many years. Following this example, Aunt Alexandra Worsley, known to her sisters as Baby, whose husband had been killed with the Royal Horse Guards in the 1st Battle of Ypres, became a Lady in Waiting to Queen Elizabeth The Queen Mother.

The twins were part of the showpiece at court functions to

which they added a note of elegance and beauty. And within the private drawing rooms of the Royal Circle at Windsor and Buckingham Palace and Sandringham they must have removed any tendency towards formality because of their buoyant high spirits and simplicity.

In 1905 my father was invited to stay at Windsor for Ascot Races. On the first evening my parents sat on opposite sides of the table and it was not until three days later that my mother and father were introduced. My father was waiting to take part in a game of golf which had been arranged to take place after the races against the Prince of Wales (later King George V). When a message came to say that the Prince had been detained, a foursome was made up in which my father was asked to play with the young Maid of Honour who happened to be waiting near the first tee, hoping for a game with another member of the Household. The game involved periods of waiting while one of the party tried to extricate himself from an awkward series of bunkers; but my father did not appear to be over-anxious to talk to my mother, and in fact kept taking out his watch, which my mother admired and about which she made some remark. She was told that the watch had been given to my father by his mother to give to his future wife. As they walked together back to the Castle, my father asked my mother to play golf the following morning. Next day after their game of golf was over they became inseparable at the races. The outcome, which took place on the last day of my father's stay, was described by my mother:

On Saturday morning we meant to play golf before breakfast as arranged, but to my surprise Douglas did not wish to play and paid off the caddies. We looked for a quiet seat but not finding one he blurted out. 'I must propose to you standing!' This was very abrupt and I must say quite unexpected, but I accepted him."

2

Childhood

My father was descended from the de Hagas, a Norman family who settled at Bemersyde in 1162. After eight generations they became Haigs. From the 13th century until Flodden they fought and died in the many battles of Independence. Thomas the Rhymer of Ercildoune was able to reassure the 4th Laird, Petrus, who was worried about the chance of his survival, with the prediction:

> "Tyde what may
> whate'er betyde
> Haig shall be Haig
> of Bemersyde."

In the 17th century Robert Haig, my forbear, son of the 17th Laird, decided to leave Bemersyde for St Ninians in Stirlingshire where he became a distiller, leaving his younger brother who had married a rich wife to carry on the property. The whisky business grew until my grandfather John, born in 1802, put it on an international footing. My father became chairman in later life but there is now no family interest.

I was born in a mock Tudor house called Eastcott on Kingston Hill on the night of 15 March 1918. My mother has written:

> "Few babies can have been so welcomed. The newspapers acclaimed him and everyone seemed to take a personal

pleasure in his arrival. Douglas returned to France the day after, but before he left he received from the King and Queen at Buckingham Palace Their Majesties' very warm congratulations."

The Germans were about to make their last great attack towards Amiens.

A few weeks later I was baptized in an improvised chapel near the house by the Chaplain General to the British Expeditionary Force, Dr John Sims. I had fourteen very distinguished godparents: The King, Lords Cambridge, Derby and French, an Indian Maharajah Sir Pratap Singh, Sir Eric Geddes who had been in charge of the railways in France, my cousin General Neil Haig and my great uncle Walter Vivian, who referred to me in a letter to my mother as the War Warrior. The list of godmothers was no less imposing, consisting of Queen Alexandra, The Empress Eugénie, widow of Napoleon III, and three of my mother's friends Mrs Cazalet, Mrs Max Wood and Mrs Fox Pitt and finally my aunt Violet Vivian.

I was indeed given a silver spoon and many beautiful mugs and cups, trays, knives and forks. Lord Derby wrote: "I am sure my godson will be worthy of his father." General Plumer, one of the donors of a beautiful silver tray inscribed with the signatures of the Army Commanders and their staffs wrote, "It will perhaps in years to come remind him of those who served under his father in this memorable war." I was duly photographed beside this tray to which I tried to add my signature with the aid of a silver pusher. That scratch is visible to this day.

My memories of pram life are hazy. I am told that the career of one of my nannies was short-lived because she had allowed herself, in her enthusiasm for the reflected glory in which I lay, to tie a placard to my pram marked "Haig's Baby" and with a Union Jack tied to the handlebars wheeled me among the other nannies in Hyde Park. When the 'flu epidemic hit our household, one of the housemaids died and I barely survived.

My parents were able to separate their public and their private lives. Perhaps the telephone was not so insidious in those days. The peace and privacy of our family life allowed me to become a much-loved, well-fed, fat, contented baby.

Eastcott was a place which my father took towards the end of the First World War to have some place for his family to live in. It was fairly close to Whitehall, near enough for him to attend conferences and meetings. We lived there until 1923. We were a happy family, two elder sisters, Xandra and Doria, and a younger sister Rene born in 1919.

I have happy memories of a visit to Queen Alexandra at Sandringham in November 1922, when my godmother took us for visits to the stables to feed carrots to the horses – her friends who meant so much to her in the solitude of her deafness. After tea my godfather, King George V, would come over to play with us on his knee: "This is the way the farmers ride". Queen Alexandra would be on the floor painting coloured cards for us of strange animals. In my mother's words, "The Queen and Miss Charlotte Knollys played with the children like two-year-olds." The Queen loved children and we loved her.

Owing to the fact that our parents were away a great deal we were sent away to visit other members of our family. Luckily these relations were themselves all fairly stable people living in comfortable homes in the country. In 1921, while our parents were in South Africa to attend the foundation conference of the British Empire Services League, we visited our Uncle George and Aunt Nancy Vivian in Cornwall. Uncle George had been severely wounded while serving in the South African war as a subaltern in the 17th Lancers of which my father was Colonel. He shared my mother's taste for parties and fun and was at his best as an entertainer. He loved dressing up in fancy dress and was always ready to produce a penny from his sleeve or mouth to surprise the young. He was a regular attender at rowing regattas on the Thames, dressed in a Leander cap, and would not have been out of place in a performance of *The Good Old Days*. There was a wonderful thrust about his gaiety as, arms akimbo, he drove his partners through the waltz at the local balls. His talent for entertainment was inherited by his son Tony who became the partner of C.B. Cochrane in a number of musicals. Though he was somewhat exhibitionist in his displays for the benefit of the children, we all had a happy time. Daphne and Tony were much older than we were, but Douglas and Vanda were near enough in age for us to be able to share many things. Later on we were to hunt in the wintertime with the Fowey Harriers of which Aunt Nancy was Master. Behind the house lay Bodmin Moor and the Jamaica Inn, the meeting place of smugglers. Across the moor when hounds ran we jumped quite large banks with surprising ease, though the occasional wall which we had to fly was more difficult. I was to be taught to shoot by Uncle George, who sat on a shooting stick ready for rabbits bolted by ferrets. Beside us were his labradors which he trained for field trials. When the River Fowey was right and a run of peel came up, he took me down to spin with spoons before the introduction of fixed spool reels. All that came later. Early memories are of his library wall plastered with big game trophies, of an old smelly dog called Raid, relic from the war, who on occasion was photographed with his medals. On visits to the pigsty, Uncle George took a sadistic pleasure in carrying me up the path behind the house to where the pigs lived in order to dangle me over those piggy eyes looking up from below. Aunt Nancy, on the other hand, was kinder. She had her feet well on the ground and was able to supply a warmth and kindness which were unobtainable from my uncle.

In 1921 my father was given the old family home, Bemersyde, by a group of subscribers who bought it from our cousin Colonel Arthur Balfour Haig. The presentation was in token of their appreciation of his services in the First World War. The house was in a bad state, full of various kinds of rot, so it was not until my birthday in 1924 that all was ready.

On our arrival Daddy met my sister Rene and me and took us down with great pride to the river and showed us a place which was going to be very much part of one's life from then on. It was a great moment.

He was a very quiet, easy-going, loving father and great fun to be with. He wasn't, I suppose, enormously communicative but he was very patient. He would love starting us off playing golf or tennis and would lob balls at us. He used to teach us to ride. He used to smarten us up sometimes rather like the rough-riding sergeant major. That was when the tough side of him came out. Clearly he wished to give us a taste of strict discipline in accordance with his own experiences in the cavalry riding school, memories of which came back to him as he stood in the field beside the kitchen garden. He shouted his commands in a tone of voice which echoed against the garden wall. Our country rides were more peaceful, and in them he explained the time and place for each pace. He always insisted that my youngest sister Rene and I should never frighten our ponies, warning us that if we did we would pay for it later by being thrown off. This injunction never seemed to save us from the inevitable fate as we paid the painful price of becoming horsemen. When one of us did fall off cantering down hill behind his awesome back, we would be greeted by the sudden disappearance of all traces of austerity from his face and good-natured laughter shone at us instead. My riding lessons had not progressed very far when the hounds met in front of the house, and I, over-confident in my ability to ride, did a practice run round the garden. My pony, excited by the hounds, broke into a gallop and deposited me on the ground in full view of the Master, huntsman and the field.

My elder sisters rode side-saddle and had a different experience which my sister Xandra describes:

"My father disapproved of ladies riding astride and insisted that his daughters, even at a young age, should ride side-saddle. He gave us special saddles that had removable pummels so that we could alternate the sides of which we rode and so did not grow with one shoulder lower than the other. Of course we found these saddles very uncomfortable on one side and the pummels had a habit of falling out, so we were rather envious of other girls who were allowed to ride astride. . . . We would have many happy days out hunting, but these days were sometimes spoilt by the long ride home. My father thoroughly disapproved of people who telephoned for their car to come and meet them with a groom to ride the horse back. I can remember looking at that merciless back rising in a trot ahead of me and longing for it to stop. If I was really desperate with a stitch in my side I would call out 'Daddy' and then at last he would stop."

When the snow came we stopped riding and took to our toboggans. My father and I made a snowman which he attacked with his usual thoroughness. Every spadeful of snow which he added to the snowman was hammered down hard until the snowman was a veritable iceberg. When the snowman was finished, my father said to me, "Whatever you do in life do it thoroughly and build solidly in the way that I have built this snowman". He adopted the same slow rather cautious approach when playing tennis and golf. He would spend many hours on the tennis court patting balls back to Rene and myself, teaching us to place our shots and not to try and slam. His approach to drawing was also painstaking and careful. My sister Xandra describes how he took her out sketching:

"We would sit on camp stools side by side drawing twisted oak trees. 'Draw more carefully. You must take more time over it,' my father would say when I was longing to go on painting. I still have the books in which are the same subjects sketched by us both. He would take me to picture galleries and he gave me my first reverence for pictures."

Drawing and painting was encouraged by both our parents, and after tea we sometimes played a drawing game called 'heads, bodies and tails'. Tea was a family meal at which our father carefully made the tea himself. Although my mother was often not well, we managed, thanks to our father's serenity, to enjoy a happy family atmosphere. At lunchtime my sisters sat on either side of him pulling his leg. We spent peaceful afternoons fishing in the Tweed and having picnics at Smailholm Tower or by the sea at Coldingham. One very special moment was when he came to say goodnight in bed on his way down to dinner. His feelings for us were deeply felt. We loved him dearly.

He was extremely happy at Bemersyde and enjoyed to the full the short time left for him to be there. Although my mother found it less congenial, she was extremely active driving her small Hillman. One day, driving near the precipitous Leader banks with Granny Vivian, a wheel came off. Luckily my grandmother remained calmly seated on the side where the wheel was and the car did not turn over. She enjoyed playing golf and riding and hunting with my father. She was often unwell and had a serious operation in the midtwenties. With her help my father was able to complete the arrangement of his war diaries and papers.

During the First World War he had recorded the day-today events in his diary which he sent back at regular intervals by King's Messenger to my mother. It is relevant to my story to explain that my father was given much strength in the knowledge that he could put all his secret fears and hopes and decisions on to paper in his diaries and in letters to my mother with complete confidence in her ability to keep them secret.

It was a help to him to know that he could share with her his innermost thoughts and knowing that my mother was quite ready to give helpful promptings from time to time.

In the flyleaf of the copy of my father's dispatches which he gave to her after the war is inscribed the following:

> "To my wife Doris in grateful recollection of all she was to me during the Great War. . . . Although she regularly received instalments to my daily diary and so knew more than those at home what was taking place at the Front, yet no one has ever been able to say 'Lady Haig told me this'!"

During his time as Commander-in-Chief my father had to bear a heavy burden of responsibility which entailed the sending of countless men to their death. All that, with his natural sensitivity and depth of feeling, must have caused him terrible inward suffering. Since then criticisms have been made by some politicians, newspaper men and military historians about his leadership. He had an almost impossible task which he carried out to the best of his ability until final victory. He has been criticized for ambitiousness and self-seeking, accusations so far from the mark about a man brought up in a simple Scottish way intent on doing his duty. Though controversies may be necessary and the work of the historians must go on so that the various details and facets of that grim war are understood, the criticisms should be based on historical facts rather than mythology.

As children we had a close friendship with the staff. The keeper Adam Rutherford took us fishing for trout and eels and was never short of a story to stimulate our interest. The chauffeur, Gillies, drove our second-hand Hudson on family picnics with smiles beaming from behind the wheel. He and his car were my chief and earliest models. I remember him tapping its mudguard in the garage to explain that the rather tinny sound indicated that the car was old. The steep brae to

our house caused overheating and we watched the thermo-
meter on the bonnet anxiously in case it boiled and we all had
to get out. My mother also drove us somewhat erratically in
a small touring Hillman. Henderson, the groom, had tattoo
marks, very penetrating blue eyes and a winning smile.
Sometimes this smile turned to anger when on the way home
from collecting the eggs the chestnut, Billy, started bucking
and the eggs were broken. My father's batman, Secrett, kept
a benevolent if wary eye on our need for entertainment. Only
on wet days were we forced to get through the day playing
with trains. I had a special favourite, a steam one that used a
methylated spirit burner to heat the water.

The grown-up world was separate from ours, and my recol-
lections of distinguished figures from the late war are few.
Isolated incidents stick in my mind. I remember the visit of
Queen Mary, when plans for a dignified reception at our
school-room door were upset by Rene's inability to retain a
balanced curtsey. The visit of Mr Churchill after a nearby
Conservative fete gave an inkling of some of the differences
which existed between the two great men.

I remember my father talking with his Chief Gunner, Sir
Noel (Curley) Birch, in our car coming back from Floors
Castle after the Conservative rally in the summer of 1927.
Churchill was trundling along in the car behind because he
was coming to tea at Bemersyde. In our car were just Sir
Noel, my father and myself, and these two Generals were
discussing Churchill's book *The World Crisis*. The part which
dealt with Passchendaele had just come out and these two
were absolutely hopping mad and the whole car practically
exploded. I can remember my father saying that Winston
really didn't know what had happened, what the problems
were and what the difficulties were over the French. I can
remember a tremendous discussion and this went on for about
nine or ten miles between Floors and Bemersyde. On arrival
my father got out and then the sun came out and my father

was his usual beaming warm self. Although Churchill had opposed my father's strategy, they had worked very closely together in the latter part of the war when my father was Commander-in-Chief and Churchill was Secretary of State for Munitions. After the war they had been responsible for the demobilization plans when Churchill was Secretary of State for War and my father was Commander-in-Chief of Home Forces. My father thought Churchill had done a good job over munitions, so in spite of their differences over strategy my father and Churchill shared a mutual respect and admiration.

I can remember very well being with him during the summer of 1925 or 1926 when we foregathered on Horse Guards for a great ex-service parade preparatory to marching down Whitehall to The Cenotaph. The Legion Patron was The Prince of Wales who was in front and we had Sir Brunel Cohen, who was the Treasurer and who had no legs, and George Crosfield, who was the National Chairman, who had one leg. I wasn't much of a marcher and of course these legless people were not very good at keeping in step and I think my father minded because The Prince of Wales wasn't really keeping in step either. We set of towards the Cenotaph at the head of this long column of men, most of whom were either on crutches or in wheelchairs.

About that time I was taken to the Wembley Exhibition in the charge of Lady Jellicoe, a strong personality. We drove in a large car with Lady Jellicoe issuing instructions through a megaphone to the chauffeur in front. On arrival she took me up to the top of a tall tower where I was launched on a mat down a spiral shute. On reaching the ground I was able to escape into the crowd in rare freedom.

Most mornings when our father was at home we used to visit him during the final stages of his dressing. One morning, seeing a pearl stud on his dressing table I slipped it in my sporran as an attractive kind of marble, and then hid it in the secret drawer of the desk which my father had used as a boy. You opened the drawer inside to release a catch which opened the secret one. I was a vague boy and very dreamy (my sisters said that one day my pony stopped to eat some grass and I went straight on), and my dreams let me do funny things. One day, when my father showing the desk to some guests, the secret catch was proudly released, the drawer popped open, and to my father's astonishment, there appeared inside it the missing pearl stud. In spite of his perplexity he did not call me a thief. I was never admonished and I hope he understood.

I spent much of my time drawing pictures of people and animals and all the things and places which surrounded me. I lived in the world of imagination, recreating the essence of ships and of horsemen and hounds, of engines and of cavalry officers mounted and in uniform. Some of my drawings were of Bemersyde and were topographically correct with the trees and flowerbeds fairly accurately placed. Others were freer in expression and design, and in these I was able to draw abstract shapes and forms according to my fantasy. I also drew people as visualized by my dolls, George and Teddy. Many of my drawings were of charabancs full of people, or of sunlit landscapes, or of houses with smoke billowing from the chimneys. My drawings of racing yachts and schooners stemmed from watching my Uncle Willie's and Aunt Henrietta's yacht *Magdalene* riding at anchor opposite the windows at St Marnocks, when I was recovering from an appendix operation, which, because it was accompanied by whooping cough, had led to complications. This had been an emergency after the pains had hit me when crossing the Irish Channel on a rough sea. Many of my drawings were of ships in which my mother journeyed on health cruises in the Mediterranean or accompanying my father to Canada or South Africa for the British Empire Services League conferences.

Because of my mother's frequent departures our emotional

ties were disrupted. Although I came to rely on my more prosaic and practical nanny, Nanny Dunn, I longed during my mother's absences for the comfort of her gentleness, and for her warmth and *joie de vivre*. Because of my unhappiness I had recourse to my inner world of fantasy and many of my childhood drawings depicted ships crossing the horizon and bore titles like 'Mummy's Ship' or 'Goodbye to the Liner'.

Although I was lonely I was not encouraged by my mother to play with the village boys. Once at a fete I entered the three-legged race with a boy whom I greatly admired and who had long trousers. Before the race had time to begin, my mother removed the hanky and sent me back to the house where, in the solitude of my room, I cried.

In the summer of 1925 my father was invited to Canada in order to attend the conference of the British Empire Services League in Ottawa and, as he had hoped, encourage the amalgamation of some fourteen Canadian ex-service organizations, whose welding together my father considered to be of paramount importance. The proposed amalgamation echoed the policy which he had already adopted in the United Kingdom, and which had led to the foundation of the British Legion. The two main organizations in Canada had in recent months been at loggerheads; the Army and Naval veterans were in the process of accusing the Great War Veterans Association of the misappropriation of wartime canteen funds – an issue which was more a question of inadequate drafting of constitutions rather than wrong spending – and this issue came at the end of a period of wrangling, an uncomfortable process for the returned soldier. There had been some opposition to my father's going on the ground that the time was not yet ripe. As my father put it, "If that is the condition of affairs, now is the time they need me". So he went. Amalgamation of the organizations proved easier than had been expected. My father faced little opposition. Having listened patiently to the various groups and addressed a large gathering of ex-servicemen whom he advised to get together, nearly everyone seemed to be ready to unite, and in November of that year the preliminaries to the formation of the Canadian Legion took place. After the conference my parents made a tour of Canada in a special train. They came home with a Red Indian head-dress and cowboy's chaps from Calgary.

The loneliness caused by this degree of isolation was becoming harmful and my parents decided to send me to boarding school. In May 1926 I was taken, aged eight, by my father to a pre-preparatory school at Westbourne House, Folkestone, run by a Mrs Hylton. To my disappointment, on the morning of our departure I was told by my father through his bathroom door that we could not leave because of the general strike. After two weeks the crisis was over and we set off. I cannot remember many incidents on the journey, although my father gave me a running commentary on places that interested him as we looked out of the window of the train. On reaching London we collected from Rowes my school clothes which included a sailor suit and an exciting lanyard and whistle. I slept in my father's bedroom and I remember seeing him naked for the first and only time in my life. Next day we travelled on to Folkestone past the Sugar Loaf Hill, which reminded him of manoeuvres when he had been a subaltern with the 7th Hussars at Shorncliffe. During the journey my father despatched a telegram each day to my mother to keep her in touch with events and to reassure her about my morale. So far this was excellent. It was only that night that the effects of homesickness struck me and I realized desperately my love for all the people, the places and the animals at home. But next day I felt better. There were many excitements, not least the putting on of the splendid long white cricket flannels and the oiling of my new cricket bat. The presence of some twenty-two other small boys and Christian Howard, the one girl, provided the first opportunity of taking part in team games. Perhaps a veil should be drawn over my performance at them, and I cannot pretend that I really enjoyed them.

More pleasurable was the way Mrs Hylton helped us to explore the worlds of flora and fauna. Football, gym, riding, cricket, went by without incident and without much thrill. At half term my father and mother came down and took me to Canterbury Cathedral, and then for a walk in a bluebell wood, followed by a meal of strawberries and cream.

Mrs Hylton had a considerable admiration for my father, and in a lesser way for Bertie Fisher, father of one of my fellow pupils and who was later to become my guardian. My father and Bertie Fisher were in her eyes faultless knights and were continually quoted as examples of men whom we should look up to. According to her, they never drank and they never smoked. I knew, however, that, though my father hated smoking, he possessed a well-stocked cellar, and that at night before dinner wine bottles were uncorked and decanted.

Mr Hylton figured mainly on the games grounds, where I was no star. He also waited at the foot of the stair as we came downstairs for breakfast. If, as sometimes happened, I came down in my gym shoes instead of my house shoes, this meant that I had used my house shoes as a chamber pot during the night, and I was duly corrected. I cannot remember his precise method of chastisement, but whatever it was it was not really painful and the problem affecting me while I was asleep came to an end. My expression in the school photograph taken during the summer term showed a mixture of innocence, charm and a touch of lurking humour. We were encouraged to sing solos in chapel. During a visit by my father to the school I was made to read the lesson and sing solo one of the verses of "To be a Pilgrim".

The following year I moved to Bramcote School in Scarborough, where Mr Pidcock prepared boys for Winchester. Ten days after term began I was operated on for a mastoid in a nursing home near the school. My parents came down and helped me through the worst. When the pain was over I enjoyed drawing horses, and someone showed me how to paint the highlights on their flanks using a purple undercoat. Later my mother wheeled me in a bath chair along the esplanade. Before returning home I had my tonsils out, and I was finally able to get back to school for the last ten days of term.

My parents were worried that because tonsils had caused my mastoid my sister Rene might suffer the same fate. So she was taken with the utmost care and kindness by my father to an Edinburgh Nursing Home for the same operation which was probably unnecessary. As my father took the view that a surgeon's knife should be avoided at all costs it is likely that it was my mother who had taken the decision.

My resistance was down. During the Christmas holidays my father took a box at the King's Theatre for a matinee performance of a pantomime. I caught paratyphoid from bad milk in the theatre and became really ill, with my mother at full nursing steam and two nurses in attendance. Towards the end of January I was well enough for my father to plan a trip abroad, and he and my mother went to stay in London en route for Nice.

On the evening of 28 January 1928 my father died suddenly in London from a heart attack while undressing to go to bed. The news was broken to me a day or so later by the nurse as my mother was still in London. My young sister Rene was now at school and I was alone. The blow hit me hard. My father was the bedrock of my security. He was my friend and I loved him deeply. His death meant the cornerstone of the family had gone. My mother was not well. My two elder sisters were competitors with each other and had never been close to my mother since their early days when they stayed with Aunt Violet because my parents were abroad in India. The one common bond between my elder sisters was their idolization of their father. Happily the following year Doria married Andrew Scott, a member of the Buccleuch family who introduced sanity and balance to the family atmosphere. His sense of humour and his humanity lifted us out of the doldrums which followed my father's death and he prevented my family from becoming too fragmented. Andrew was supported by his cousin Walter Dalkeith, later Duke of Buccleuch, who lived on the other side of the river below the Eildons. To Walter more than anyone else I owe the guidance which was so necessary after my father's death. He taught me to shoot and, though strict, he was always kind. It was he who gave me some discipline in preparation for my military life ahead. He had three children a little younger than Rene and myself, of whom Elizabeth Scott, my secret love, was the elder, followed by Johnnie and Caroline. After the war Elizabeth married someone else, an event which was to mar my happiness for some time. Mollie Dalkeith was very kind to us. She was at her best with children. She loved building bonfires and looking for blackberries and mushrooms. She loved the furniture, silver and paintings in the houses which she would inherit.

So far as our own family affairs were concerned my mother became gradually more detached, and responsibilities for running our house during the holidays fell increasingly into the hands of my sister Doria. For her practical care I will always be grateful. Finance at the Trust end was administered by Trevor Castle of the Public Trustee Office and at the Bemersyde end by Major David Burns of the British Linen Bank in St Boswells. I had not yet acquired the four let farms, so the size of the estate was small, and the Trust income seemed adequate to pay for maintenance and the cost of our limited staff, together with the cost of my school bills.

3

Schooldays

When the news of my father's death was broken to me as I lay in bed suffering from paratyphoid, the papers were shown to me. I became aware of his greatness, of his lifelong public service, and that he belonged not just to his family but to the Nation.

In the papers I now saw photographs of long queues of people waiting to file past his coffin lying in state at St Columba's. I saw how the coffin was taken on 3 February by gun carriage to Westminster Abbey. Solemn photographs of the procession moving through London showed the flag-draped coffin escorted by Marshals Foch and Pétain from France, Baron de Ceuninck from Belgium and eleven British war leaders, followed by his charger – his boots reversed – accompanied by his batman, Secrett. Behind marched the Prince of Wales, the Duke of York, Prince Henry and Prince Arthur of Connaught at the head of a vast concourse of slow-marching men.

From Westminster Abbey the coffin was taken to Waterloo, and as the train moved out his charger neighed a farewell salute. When the coffin returned to Scotland my mother could also come home, accompanied by my two elder sisters. As she came in to the room our eyes met and she was able to share some of her grief with me. Her coming home and her descriptions made the funeral photographs more real and, being close to her, I felt less alone and I was able to share with her from my bed the descriptions of what had happened. I was able too to help her answer some of her many letters of condolence, many of them from old comrades who had served with my father. Others I sent on to Colonel Crosfield, Chairman of the Legion, with a covering letter: "I am writing for Mummy and sending you the enclosed letters which came recently for Daddy, and please would you attend to them? Mummy asked me to do this as she is so busy."

Meanwhile the funeral train had arrived at the Caledonian Station in Edinburgh. It drew in in silence at midnight. Only the clinking of the horses' bits of two squadrons of The Greys was heard as the train came to a halt. Crowds of people waited in homage to welcome him on his last return to his native city. Soldiers from The Royal Scots Greys, the 2nd Battalion Cameron Highlanders and The London Scottish escorted the gun carriage up the slippery slopes of the hill past the Castle to St Giles. The night was clear moonlight and it was freezing hard.

For three days the coffin lay in state in St Giles while Scotsmen and women filed past in homage. Then the funeral cortège moved on once more escorted by The Greys and Cameron Highlanders from St Giles Cathedral to Waverley Station whence the coffin was taken by train to St Boswells.

My father had expressed the wish to be buried in the family burial ground in Dryburgh Abbey rather than in St Paul's. So it was in the peaceful Abbey grounds beside the River Tweed that he found his last resting place. The ceremony was a simple one. The hierarchy of the church were excluded and only Mr J.F. McCreath, Minister of Mertoun Church, of which my father had been an Elder, took the service. No troops took part except for a small detachment of trumpeters from The Greys and pipers from the 4th Battalion of The King's Own Scottish Borderers to sound the Last Post and Reveille. The coffin moved slowly on a farm cart escorted by pall bearers from the Bemersyde estate and by members of the Border Area of the British Legion Scotland. Only the bright colours of the Union Jack and the poppy wreaths relieved the sombre black of the mourners who took part in this simple ceremony gathered among the ruins of the Abbey. After the funeral was over the family was left among the trees and the snowdrops at Bemersyde.

My father's death was an emotional blow of an enormous kind, a sort of psychological blow which probably affected me forever. I was much too young when he died, of an age when it is very important to have a father. My mother wasn't very well afterwards and she had a lot of strains and stresses, including financial difficulties. None of my father's director-ships came any more, nor indeed any of his pay, and we were saddled with a large house and lots of servants and inadequate money to pay them with. So most of the servants had to go, and we really had to cut down. It was a cold wind that started blowing.

I cannot remember much about the days following my father's funeral. The house seemed empty. I was confined to a bedroom in the east wing and for a few days my elder sisters, dressed in black, came and sat with me and we listened to records of songs by Frank Crumit on the gramophone. The rooks were beginning to build their nests in the beech trees outside, and Sister Richardson, my hospital nurse, came back from her walks with presents of snowdrops for my room. I was given a new companion, my father's terrier, Gyp, who would share my life until I left for the war eleven years later.

My mother must have been kept busy making readjust-ments and alterations which would have repercussions on our way of life. Pitt, the butler, whose pale complexion showed the effects of a gas attack at Loos, was asked to leave and with him went the footman and the hall boy. Secrett, my father's batman for thirty years, had already left before my father's death. So our household was considerably reduced. Soon after getting up I handed to each member of the staff his weekly wage. There were still three gardeners of whom the youngest got ten shillings a week.

My mother was determined to carry on my father's work for the Legion and for ex-service people. She decided to open the tower to the public, not for profit but to raise money for her Poppy Factory in Edinburgh and to enable my father's home to become a shrine for ex-service pilgrims from all over the world. She put together all his mementoes, uniforms, decorations, freedom caskets and maps in three rooms in the tower where he had worked and slept.

The drawing room was shrouded in dust sheets and the front hall became the main living room. A screen shielded us from the gaze of the public as they paid their entrance at the front door and prepared to climb the spiral stair. Any particularly indiscreet remark by a member of the family was apt to receive an echoing cough from the guide who was stationed, bowler-hatted, on the other side of the screen. My mother's energy and mind became focused on a hectic programme of Legion functions and during her free time at Bemersyde she began to prepare a book about my father's life.

As soon as I was able to get out of bed and begin to recuperate (I had spent some twelve weeks in bed) I was armed with a Latin grammar and books of poetry and maths. With stern resolution, my mother was determined that I make up for lost time. Because my illness had left me with a weak heart I could not go back to school; so a tutor was engaged, a parson, who was something of a pervert who enjoyed lowering my trousers for corporal punishment whenever my slow brain failed to remember the lines. The beatings were quite hard so I told my mother and the man was dismissed. A friend of my mother's, Miss Florence Horsburgh, later Minister of Education, then taught me for a while with more patience and understanding than that of her predecessor.

I spent some time each morning with my mother as she lay in bed, talking about my father's life and career. Her praise and admiration were unqualified. In her eyes he was greater than Wellington, greater than Marlborough. She was determined to inspire in me some of the sense of duty and the humility which were his. The picture she painted assumed a powerful if unreal force in my life and imbued me with worship and admiration for an ideal almost saint-like father figure.

After my father's death I had received a message from the troop of scouts and cubs at the Richmond Poppy Factory, the boys whom he had inspected and addressed on the day before his death, when he had called on them always to speak up for their King and country.

"From the scoutmaster, cubmaster and boys of the 20th Richmond (Earl Haig's Own) troop BP Scouts as a token of their good wishes and prayers that you may soon be restored to health, and of their pride at numbering you among the members of their pack and at having you as one of their brother Wolfcubs.

Cyril Howe
Group Scoutmaster"

As soon as I was well enough to travel I was enrolled as "Cub Dawyck" in "Earl Haig's own pack". A newspaper report described how "the great soldier's son, a slim lad with splendid eyes, was made an honorary pack leader and promised to be loyal and do his duty to God and the King".

In her speech my mother said that "her son had not merited the honour of being made pack leader, nor the three stripes which had been conferred on him, but had received them because of his father's work. He in turn had to work to deserve them, and she hoped and was sure that she would not be disappointed that in the course of his life, he might win many stripes."

During the summer I was also taken to visit my sister Rene,

who, dressed in chocolate-coloured uniform was at school at Duncombe Park in Yorkshire. When we got there my sister took one look at me and then abandoned me, leaving me alone among a lot of sniggering girls while she went off to prepare to take her part as Minnehaha in *Hiawatha*. Luckily by September I was considered by the doctors to be well enough for school. Instead of Bramcote my mother now chose Cargilfield near Edinburgh on the grounds that it was nearer home than my original school at Scarborough and because of its greater protection from the North Sea. British preparatory schools have never been recognized for their comforts nor for any degree of cosiness between the boys, though, no doubt, as I had seen at Duncombe Park, the atmosphere in the girls' equivalent was far from perfect. Nevertheless Cargilfield in those days was tough, far tougher than it is today when new boys are encouraged to arrive with teddy bears to keep them company. I recognized at once its toughness in comparison to the friendlier atmosphere of Bramcote where I had been among friends and even found admirers willing to waste time watching me draw horses. I had gone to Bramcote on an equal footing with the others and, though I was no lover of football, was able to play rugger and run like them. Now because of my weak heart rugger was forbidden and when lunch was over, instead of being allowed to change and run about the football ground with the others, I was left alone to while away the afternoon with my mashie and putter. This inability to participate at games and my exoneration from the morning cold bath together with the grand title printed in front of my name on the school list generated a kind of envy among my fellows who had never come across a live Earl before. Their jealousy about my title and about my privileges caused them to stop me in the passage, to goad me and torment me and even add a kick for good measure. I was a welcome target for bullying and, because of my recent sheltered sickroom existence and of my trusting nature, my powers of retaliation were weak. My name was later changed to plain initials on the list. This was because my mother had conveyed her concern which on this occasion was fully justified, although on other occasions was less so, when for example the poor matron was sacked at her behest for putting poultices on too hot. To help me pass the time I was given an allotment in the grounds where for a while I became a keen grower both of annuals and perennials. The headmaster, Mr Wallace, a big powerful giant who had retired from the Police service in India, and was later to become Bishop of Exeter, once a week, booted and spurred, took me to a riding school in Edinburgh where he mounted a huge horse on which, with me following on a pony, he lumbered along Queensferry Road. Mr Wood Smith, his senior master, was also kind and helped me fly a model aeroplane and in winter gave parties in his room with hot chestnuts and cocoa. My mother was prone to arrive unexpectedly to see me without regard for school hours and regulations. I remember her sad face waiting in her car by the door into the Ash Court and sensed her emotional need to be near me.

When Armistice time came, the first since my father's death, in spite of the intention not to differentiate me from the other boys I was made to lay a wreath on the War Memorial in the Canongate. After the service I returned to school with my mind full of the singing of "Onward Christian Soldiers". My mother's mind focused on the Poppy Factory and on the disabled workers. She filled our home with Factory products; old 78 gramophone records heated and shaped into flower vases with the holes plugged up, various kinds of drawing room bric-à-brac, ash trays in the form of painted wooden poppy heads mounted on supports, lampstands and coffee tables (rather more useful than beautiful). Luckily on my days out from school, which were on Sundays, the Factory was closed, but that did not stop my mother driving me instead to visit the disabled men in Edenhall Hospital or to see them at home recuperating after an operation or amputation. Looking back to the early days of the Factory, it is fair to say that the amount of disablement was greater than it is today. My memories are of terribly handicapped men, many of them on crutches and in wheelchairs. Every Christmas we were driven up to the Factory to attend the annual children's party and once in summertime a bus party of factory members visited us at Bemersyde when with tremendous spirit a legless man climbed up the spiral staircase to the top of the Peel Tower.

The special aura of church, of wreaths of poppies, figures in dark clothes standing at attention whilst singing the National Anthem at the foot of war memorials was unreal. At times, when my mother was ill or unable to see me, I was taken out by Dr Charles Warr, Dean of the Thistle, a cheerful human man who let me drive his car surreptitiously on the drive at home. But even the warmth of his address from the Pulpit could not disperse the gloom of the Manse Pew in St Giles where I was made to sit instead of going home like the other boys to rag and play. One Sunday in the year following my father's death – it was 1929 – I took part in a solemn service of dedication to the Shrine of Youth when, in the presence of the Lord Provost and representatives of Scottish Youth organizations, I carried the Banner of the Order of the Bath, which had belonged to my father, in the procession and placed it into the safe custody of the Dean.

Because of the cold in the dormitories where in winter the water jugs froze because there was no heating, my resistance was low and when measles struck the school it struck me doubly hard. I was sent home, where my mother, as usual at her best when family illness approached, had prepared the East Wing as a sick room, rigging up disinfected sheets to isolate the germs from the rest of the house. Almost at once pneumonia set in and two hospital nurses were sent for to look after me. A steam tent was erected. As I lay ill and exhausted with a high fever the tent collapsed and the heater set light to my bed from which I crawled to safety. Hearing cries from the room below the nurse emerged to spray Minimax not only on the bed but on the pictures and furniture as well.

I soon recovered, thanks to good food cooked by Mrs McLeod, and after the holidays rejoined Cargilfield with my heart stronger, and thus able to play cricket and later rugger like the others. I felt much happier under the new head-master, J.H. Bruce Lockhart, whose arrival heralded an artistic renaissance. Creativity spread through all depart-ments; there was less drawing from cones and cylinders and plaster casts of feet and hands. Each day at lunchtime every boy was made to listen to one side of a seventy-eight record of Beethoven immediately following the moment when debtors (those who had failed to visit the lavatory that day) put up their hands so that their names could be put on the laxative list. At the end of the spring term *Iolanthe* was put on, elaborately produced with cardboard coronets and false ermined robes. I found myself in the part of Lord Tolloller. "Bow bow ye lower middle classes" was marvellous to sing, though I was not clear what the words really meant. Poetry linocutting, carpentry and a more exciting school magazine were all threads in the stimulating new tapestry woven by the Bruce Lockharts and part of a general happiness which I was able to enjoy for nearly two years until the time came for me to pass quite easily the common entrance examination for Stowe.

This school was chosen by my mother with reluctant support from my guardian Bertie Fisher, because of its progressiveness and lack of austerity. Owing to my illness I had been considered too backward to try for Winchester, the choice of my father who had vetoed Eton for its snobbery. Before I left Cargilfield the Headmaster, whose insight had encouraged me to enjoy the excitement of the three-quarter line, advised me to concentrate as far as possible on the arts rather than on games. He had the right to advise, since he himself was good at both. He was a gifted painter and a rugger international as well.

My elder sisters had now left home. Xandra went to live in London and Doria had married Andrew Scott soon after our father's death. Their wedding took place in the summer of 1929 in Mertoun Kirk, where, as they emerged from the service, their first few steps of shared happiness were made through an arch of crutches held over their head in military fashion by members of the Poppy Factory.

In consequence of our elder sisters' irregular visits and because our mother was not well, Rene and I were left to our own devices. Our mother's somewhat mobile if erratic way of life and many responsibilities made it necessary for her to live in Edinburgh as well as at Bemersyde. She was often ill and, since our home was closed during the term time, Rene and I encountered a series of temporary servants, of tutors, and numbers of helpers, too many to be described here, who acted as custodians and guides on our mother's behalf. Without proper leadership some of the outdoors staff left and instead a number of retired officers, unlucky perhaps because of individual failings, tried their hand as groom or chauffeur, tasks for which they were not fitted.

My mother was no fool, so their position was not secure. She encouraged Rene and me to meet many friends in the Borders, as well as to invite friends from further away, whom she treated as strictly as she did us.

I went to Stowe for the Summer term 1931. Dressed in a smart grey flannel suit and homburg hat, accompanied by my mother, I arrived at Bletchley station where we were met by a chauffeur in a maroon livery with silver buttons, driving a maroon Humber belonging to the Headmaster, J.F. Roxburgh, and driven up the long drive to the Adam house which had been the home of the Dukes of Buckingham.

I relaxed in the warmer, freer climate of Stowe. I enjoyed

the peace of the woods and fields, and fished in the lakes and slow streams. Instead of cricket and rugger I concentrated on fencing, tennis and riding. At a slower pace and in a more congenial atmosphere my health picked up. My soul responded to the beauty of the park, its temples and monuments, and the sensitivity of J.F. I was encouraged once or twice a term to hunt with Bear Hillingdon, Master of the Grafton, who lent me a pony and gave me tea after long rides home. As we rode up to Wakefield Lodge in the dusk the Master blew his horn and the yards became alive with scurrying men opening stable doors and clanking pails. Much of my school life was centred on dogs and horses and the fields around. My housemaster was Richard Haworth, nicknamed Chin, a retired regular Major who had been severely wounded at Gallipoli whilst serving with the Lancashire Fusiliers. He was a distant father figure who in spite of his military background – he had been a Company Commander at Sandhurst – did not rule us with a rod of iron. I remember, having been caught smoking while packing in the dormitory, being beaten by him. Afterwards as I left feeling my aching bottom, I touched the broken pieces of my fountain pen which was in the back pocket of my trousers. Furious, I went back to report my find. "Damn cheek," was all Chin said. "Bend over again," and gave me two more strokes. His house was mainly composed of the sons of poorly endowed Army officers. Some of us owned whippets with which we roamed the country after hares. Sometimes when funds were there we bicycled to Buckingham for a bottle of gin or sherry, stopping *en route* to light a cigarette.

One day, pedalling with two companions along the drive to Buckingham, I saw them stop and put their bikes against a tree. Then, to my surprise, one of them, a Bishop's son, fell upon the other. That was the only homosexual occasion that I remember, though I had some advances made to me on a sofa by a master during private history lessons. Chin had warned me about the problems of buggery and it is fair to say that in his time homosexuality was not uncommon.

In the main our interests and pleasures were innocent. Our mentalities were pure and we shared a comradeship and an enjoyment of lives which would in too many cases be cut short by the war. Because of our military backgrounds most of us were to join up when the war began and too many of us had their names inscribed on the war memorial. At that time we were a happy band enjoying the light-hearted comradeship of OTC camps.

I had many friends but no close ties except perhaps with Tim Llewellyn Palmer, who hid a wild and choleric streak beneath a saintlike smile. At his home at Rushmore some thirty horses ran wild in the park. He kept a ponytrap – 'the chubby cart' – in which he raced through the woods regardless of obstacles. His character was strong, too strong according to our housemaster. The latter was sometimes green and morose as on one occasion when Sergeant Radice, a somewhat untidy and unmilitary figure, was dismissed from the OTC as being no longer worthy of wearing His Majesty's uniform for burning the Union Jack in the Assembly Hall on Empire Day. Poor Radice had had to do further penance by being publicly ducked in Cobham Pond. The masters who might have protected him remained absent, whilst hundreds of boys' heads craned from courtyard windows just as the faces must have watched the guillotine in the Place de la Concorde.

The bicycling we did, and we were allowed to cover many miles to a maximum distance of sixteen miles from the school, was part of the liberal programme laid down by the Headmaster. There were few school regulations and no traditions to hem us in and make us 'kowtow' to the past. So long as we were well mannered and remembered to take our hands out of our pockets whenever we passed a master, we had absolute freedom. Whilst we were encouraged to behave and act without the inhibitions of a traditional establishment, we were left with a greater responsibility for our own behaviour and discipline came much more from within than without. J.F.'s understanding of boys was shrewd and kind. He realized that at school our minds and our characters would have their chance to grow. He was interested in the personal make up and interests of each small boy that arrived on the north front steps. Like the gardener with green fingers who realizes this plant needs this, and that plant needs that, he watched us all, gave each one his friendship so that I think we all each one of us felt J.F. belonged to us personally and we trusted him as he trusted us and in the main neither was let down.

Every term Bertie Fisher came down to see me, when, after a session in my housemaster's room, we set off to lunch with some retired officer friend living in the neighbourhood. To reach our destination it was my duty or part of my training to mapread our way and invariably we got lost and my guardian became irritated. In his shy and diffident manner he was trying to mould me in ways that were not part of my nature and his lack of humour did not help matters for either of us. Though he appeared to me as a gentle man he was remote and somewhat frightening and could not hide from me his sense of irritation each time I failed to come up to the standards he expected of me. As I became less and less sure of myself I blundered more and more. Once he took me to France to attend the unveiling of two memorials at Arras and Thiepval, a visit which had been arranged thanks to the thoughtfulness of the Prince of Wales who had written to my mother in July 1932:

"As it is, as far as we know, the last memorial of the Great War to be unveiled in France, I think it would be a fine thing if your boy could be present, and I am sure that every soldier who fought under your distinguished husband would appreciate the presence of his son and heir.

"If you will agree with my suggestion, it will enable him

in after life to remember having taken part in a ceremony so closely associated with his father's great work in France."

Among the party was the architect who designed the Thiepval Memorial, Sir Edwin Lutyens, who taught me to draw horses in the back of the bus.

One of our masters was the music master, Dr Huggins, who had won an MC in the First World War, and who was able to combine the roles of schoolmaster and field master of the Grafton. Sometimes he took choir practice in full hunting dress beneath his gown, his hunting boots echoing on the chapel floor. Once, while giving me a piano lesson, he was astonished that I could sing top F, which he believed to be a school record. Dr Huggins helped me with lessons on music appreciation and later to be a horn player in the orchestra. All that led towards an understanding of and love for music.

Under the art master, Herbert Neville, I learnt the techniques of watercolour painting through copying the reproductions of Cotman. Later under the guidance of his successors, Robin and Dodie Watt, I was encouraged to be freer in my approach and to draw from the live model. By rigging up coloured materials behind bowls of fruit, I developed a colour sense. I also drew caricatures for the school magazine, using as my subject my housemaster, who symbolized for me an earlier theme – the soldier with sword and military moustache on horseback or on foot.

So far as school work was concerned my main purpose in working was to pass examinations. T.H. White, the author of *The Sword in the Stone*, helped me to write English and introduced me to the work of Henry Williamson. I was not interested in science and I hated maths, so that, although I got seven credits, because of my failure in maths, I failed to pass the School Certificate on the first attempt. Typically the Headmaster gave me a travelling clock as a consolation prize, and with his encouragement I was successful at maths on the second attempt and also passed with credit in English, Geography, Latin, French and Drawing.

Quite often in the holidays we went to Wales to visit Aunt Violet where the peaceful routine was sometimes broken because of the inevitable rift between the twin sisters. My mother loved dashing me off for a game of golf or swimming dangerously far out into the sea. Once, unwisely, we brought our dogs, and next day my mother's dog, a Yorkshire terrier called Puff, was killed with one bite from my Uncle Walter's retriever under the table at lunch. My mother left quite soon after the incident. Poor great uncle Walter had tried hard to preserve the peace between his nieces with no avail. He was proud of Aunt Violet, who kept house for him, and we admired his cars, a Bentley, a Sunbeam and a Star, all bright orange, which he never drove above 30 mph. During spells of fine weather we had tea beside the stream in Aunt Violet's rock garden or, when it was really settled, on the terrace over-looking the bay, where we caught our lobsters and at low tide searched the seaweed for prawns. Aunt Violet presided at tea in a cotton pinafore and an elegant tweed cap worn at a jaunty angle. After tea was over she sat doing needlework with her pug snoring on her lap.

Sometimes we spent our holidays with the Dalkeiths at Eildon, where I learnt the business of walking in line after hares and partridges or in winter standing waiting for the odd driven pheasant. Restless and energetic himself, Walter expected the same constant standard of keeness among his guns. Later he started training me on the grouse moors. Sometimes his urgent hailing from a distant hilltop was un-intelligible and I did my best to decipher the various interpretations offered by the intervening guns and keepers before deciding the best way in my slow manner to follow his instructions. One day after a stressful scene I went upstairs to change, when I heard a tap on my door and saw Walter holding a glass of champagne to cheer me up, a typical example of his care and thought. This thoughtfulness was extended towards people of all walks of life, many of them connected with his huge estates, which he managed with great thoroughness in addition to his many other duties.

During my last year at Stowe I studied German and French for the Higher Certificate in which I was successful. In his last report J.F. wrote that, though he could not forecast a career of great distinction, he could at least rely on me never to disgrace my fellows. I left Stowe in December 1935 with memories of J.F. reciting Lamartine with all its nuances expressed with the deepest feeling. I remembered the panache of his silk ties and scented handkerchiefs tucked in a nonchalant way into the pockets of his double-breasted suits. Such memories were part of a new awareness of beauty. The beauty of Stowe which had inspired J.F. had been passed on through him to our minds. Something of the Greek aesthetic canons and of the laws of harmony which governed the architectural design of Stowe crept into our thought and action. Through our environment and through the example of J.F., our minds lifted to realms of grace and understanding and balance which do not normally exalt dwellers on this earth in the twentieth century. Through our environment we found a detachment and a balance which was as great an asset as any academic qualification. In his final speech to the leavers J.F. said, "Above all, don't fall in love. If you do, depart by the next train."

With these bachelor's words of advice in our minds we left.

4

Munich and Oxford

In the New Year of 1936 my sister Rene and I spent six
months in Munich, Rene at a girls' finishing school, myself
with a German family. I learnt to speak German and I
attended an art school for the life class. I enjoyed myself
boarding trams and puffing German cigars. The latticed
windows of my bedroom, which was a focal point of my new
home at Hesse Strasse 5, gave me an impression of the
German mind. The Stengel family, with whom I stayed, were
poor and lived a frugal life. My bath was run for me each
morning by the maid with barely enough hot water to fill a
kettle. Below me the elder daughter, Lieslott, practised her
violin. Lieslott had an intelligence and charm which attracted
her to Levin Gumpenberg who later became administrative
head of all the national museums and properties in Bavaria.
During the war in 1944 I was to pass through a POW transit
camp at Moosburg, near Munich, and, being one of those
detailed to unload the baggage from the train which had
taken us from our camps in Italy, I managed to send a note to
the Stengels via our engine driver, who was an anti-Nazi. A
few days later Levin, then a corporal in the German army and
serving in our camp, who had been rung up by the Stengels,
found me and told me to give him more messages. These
messages brought Lieslott and Levin together and soon after
they were married. All this would happen later. But in 1936,
apart from the warning sound of marching soldiers in the

street outside, we were left free to live the carefree existence of cloud-cuckoo land. It was the social season of *Fasching*. There were gay parties, and some very starchy ones, in German homes and hotels. There were enough English girls at finishing schools to make the few English males in great demand and we went often to listen to Wagner at the Opera House or on skiing trips to the mountains. We left at 4 am carrying our skis through the streets. We travelled fourth class in packed trains to a small station near Garmisch, where I was left on the slopes by the line to cope with my skis while my friends went off up the mountain. I met a congenial friend from Silesia, Georg Deym, whom I saw frequently until his death fifty years later. Thanks to him I grew to love Germany and through him I was taken to many country houses belonging to his friends and relations.

Just as at Stowe I found peace and enchantment in its woods and lakes, I now enjoyed the wider vistas of Upper Bavaria and the Alps. We sailed on the lakes of Starnberg, the Chiemsee and the Königsee from where we could look up towards Berchtesgaden. Happily, at that time my mind was oblivious of its menacing future. Rather than getting involved with political matters I made the most of the gap period between school and Oxford. Just as young gentlemen from Scotland and England had enjoyed the grand tour in early generations I was able to taste some of the pleasures of visiting museums and galleries at Naumburg, Augsburg and Nymphenburg. We explored Rococo churches and the various palaces built by the mad King Ludwig.

My host Baron Stengel was a civil servant with no strong political views and, apart from meeting Reichstadt-halter Ritter von Epp, an ex soldier in the Hindenburg tradition who had been given a nominal position by Hitler in 1933, I made no Nazi contacts. Hitler's offer to von Epp had included the promise of promotion to the rank of General. This cunning bait enabled Hitler to obtain nominal support from a member of the upper class who had a good record as a soldier and who was a patriot who had served in the First World War and against the Communists in the Weimar Republic. Perhaps out of vanity, von Epp clung to all the trappings afforded to him by the Nazis in his official position until the end of the war. When he finally decided to stand against Hitler he was condemned to death but he was too exalted a member of the Nazi Party to be shot; so he was transferred to prison in Salzburg where he was eventually taken prisoner by the allies. He died in a Munich hospital as a prisoner of war at the end of 1946.

I lunched with Martin Aufhaüser, head of the Jewish Aufhaüser Bank in Munich who was later taken to Dachau in 1938. Aufhaüser was always smart in London suits, Lock hats and Lobb Shoes, these soon to be transformed into a concentration camp uniform. I also met Count Arco, the assassin of the communist Eisner at one of the Fasching Balls. One Easter time I stood in the crowd outside the Frauenkirche and listened to the applause for Crown Prince Rupprecht who had commanded an army group against my father on the Western Front. After my father's death the Crown Prince, as the Stuart Pretender to the British throne, had paid a tribute to him. He said, "I am proud to think that Haig is a Scot". I saw Hitler twice, once at the Luitpold ice rink, where his favourites, Maxie Herber and Ernst Baier, were skating, and once at Garmisch when he was watching the Olympic Games with Unity Mitford.

The Nazi movement had not yet reached its full momentum. The German middle classes were by then under Hitler's diabolical influence but no one really knew what was in store nor the reality of the concentration camps. They saw what they thought were the good sides – how prosperity had been restored and how pride returned with hard work. "*Kraft durch Freude*" was a good slogan and young people in Labour Corps Camps enjoyed working in forests or on the roads. The swastika became a symbol for good rather than evil. The people were glad to give a Nazi salute as they passed the Feldherrn Halle. They were impressed by the great Mercedes staff cars around the Brown House and by the Nazi art gallery built to house the official artists, while the work of the "degenerates" – Klee, Kandinsky and Nolde – was confiscated and burnt. They were impressed by the arms build-up and by the number of soldiers of all kinds who thronged the streets and the cafés. They visited the Army Museum and other museums built to glorify the Aryan race. If my father had been alive he would have known what was to come, as he did when he warned that war would recur once he knew the strictness of the terms of the Treaty of Versailles. That spring Hitler was already on the march across the Rhine. France, who had been the architects of the harsh peace, reacted strongly but without support from us. So Hitler got away with it and his popularity grew. Munich was the birthplace of Nazism and great crowds listened to Hitler's angry demands for a redress of the wrongs of Versailles and the means to satisfy the need for *lebensraum*. The workers on the country estates belonging to the friends of Georg seemed oblivious of the situation, but their masters, the aristocrats, were uneasy and talked gloomily about the future. Georg hated the Nazis. He was to marry a Jewish girl. At that time, still able to live modestly on private means, he refused to take up an architect's career because of the Nazis. Later, when war came, he served, fought and was left for dead in Russia, was wounded again in France, but refused ever to become an officer. He formed part of the small minority of Germans who remained steadfastly anti-Nazi. But he was part of a group which was not strong enough to disrupt the Nazis. Even if Hitler had been killed, his government would have gone on, and it was only through war that it could finally be overthrown.

So it was with Hitler's hysterical voice rising to a crescendo in the background that Rene and I went home, stopping for a few weeks on the way at Strobl to stay with our sister Xandra near the White Horse Inn. Here the Austrians indulged in a last mad whirl of gaiety, dancing Viennese waltzes in lederhosen and dirndls; and at dusk on the Traun I caught enough huge trout to provide fishing memories during the years ahead.

I had broken my Munich stay in April to come home to sit the Christ Church entrance examination which I passed. I duly arrived at Oxford in October 1936.

At Sandhurst my father had won the Sword of Honour. At Oxford he had only read for a pass degree, had enjoyed his hunting, his games of polo and had taken life easily. I followed suit. I hunted, I played polo and I was elected to the Bullingdon, a social club which had been in existence since the days of the gentlemen commoners in the eighteenth century. There I found King, still an old club retainer nearly sixty years after my father's day.

I went up to Christ Church to begin a life which was part of another century. I found myself among new faces, mostly from Eton, the faces of a generation who had come up ready to savour the graces of a patrician way of life. Our academic ambitions were not great but we learnt the art of living. We explored our tastes. We found our personal response, our choice of friends and occupations.

I lived in rooms beneath Tom Tower, whose bell tolling the hours made my bed rock. Across the quad figures flitted round Mercury towards the Cathedral and the Hall beyond. Here on non-hunting days I "sported my oak" and tried to concentrate on books. I studied French literature under the guidance of my modern languages tutor, Frank Taylor, who had lost a leg in the war and had a sensitive ear for the niceties of French pronounciation. I attended lectures on Goethe and Schiller given by Dr Stahl. During the following spring vacation John Cripps and I stayed with the de Juge family near Toulouse in order to practise French, which helped me in the summer to pass the two modern language groups needed for my preliminary degree. These were French and German. Madame de Juge was English. They had two pretty daughters, the eldest of whom, Lala, was married to a rather selfish Englishman with a wooden leg about whom Monsieur de Juge used to complain on our regular morning rides.

The art of being able to work and play, to hunt and to read, required an intellectual discipline which others like Peter Wood, Robin Hastings and Hugh Trevor-Roper were better at than I. I found myself hunting either on foot with the Christ Church Beagles or with the Warwickshire Hounds, who, according to the terms of the late Lord Willoughby de Broke's Will, invited undergraduates to hunt for nothing. From Cyril Darby of Radway I bought a small Irish six-year-old gelding called Hitler, a name given to him because he was said to be dark and bad-tempered. Hitler was a wonderful performer and I rode him in a cross-country contest in October against a Stowe team led by Marcus Lyon. *Horse and Hound* had an account:

> "Amongst the best individual performances of the afternoon were those put up by two young horsemen to whom a natural aptitude for the game has evidently descended from their respective fathers; for the late Field Marshal Earl Haig was noted as a horseman before he became otherwise famous, while Major W.E. Lyon, the well known writer on equine subjects, needs no further introduction."

My partner in the pairs was Peter Wood, who was to lose his life in the Western Desert. He wrote a series of sardonic poems for the *Isis*. In one of them, "Advice to a Freshman", he wrote:

> Be gentle in your ways and remember
>   never gaze on the wine when it is red,
> You must study all the day and when

47

your books are put away you must
quietly go to bed . . .
You must never drive a motor, wear a
tweed suit or a boater or disport a
non club tie,
Attend at local races or go riding steeple
chases for that shows you do not try
For the things that really matter such as
intellectual chatter or a good first class degree.

Peter was President of Loders Club, which had been originally
founded for Bible reading on Sunday nights. Though I and
most of my friends lived strictly austere and very innocent
lives so far as women were concerned, we managed to indulge
in wine and song, and our President was well able to lead the
singing followed by energetic climbing round the walls along
the picture rail. I was elected junior member, and as such was
responsible for finishing the port. Every Sunday night I forced
myself to down a large silver cupful of cheap port, staggered
home drunk, to feel ill for six days till the following Sabbath.
In the course of my determined effort to do my duty, I also
fell foul of the law. The President, took a heartless pleasure
in my suffering and wrote a ballad:

There once was a Proctor, a bonny wee Proctor
A-pricking his way down the High and the Turl
When his bulldogs so canny all shouted Wee Mannie
(The name of the Proctor) we view a drunk Earl.
Hoots Toots, mon, you're leein', ha' done with your speein'.
It isn't the Earl but some stour in the street.

There were evenings at Campion Hall or dinner parties in my
rooms, where on one occasion during a visit from my friend
Paul Maze, who had come down to paint the rowing during
Eights Week, there was a discussion on painting. While

Father D'Arcy described the spiritual ecstasy of the great Crucifixion paintings, Paul Maze maintained that he found a greater spirituality in a carcass of beef painted by Rembrandt.

Our social life was energetic. On two or three evenings a week during the summer we went to deb dances, and I remember going with my sister Rene to parties at Derby House and Londonderry House and to a Court Ball at Buckingham Palace, where I wore knee breeches, silk stockings and buckled shoes. The occasion was marked by the appearance of a crooner on the stage in front of the orchestra. The King seemed delighted, but Queen Mary looked shocked as she listened to the blonde girl doing her best to alleviate the stiff formality of the function. When asked for a reason why he had permitted this new venture, the Lord Chamberlain explained that he thought a crooner was an instrument not a person.

The Court Ball followed after the coronation of King George VI. I was one of the Pages of Honour to the King and to prepare for it we were involved in a series of rehearsals at Westminster Abbey. Once, at the final rehearsal, when His Majesty was present in person, my train was delayed and I arrived late at the Abbey. The doors were shut and when I was at last let in I was reprimanded by the King's Equerry, a Naval captain who really knew how to curse. Memories of the great day are vivid still. The State Coach arrived. My fellow pages – near relatives of courtiers and of great war leaders, George Jellicoe, Sandy Ramsay, Henry Kitchener and George Lascelles among them – walked in slow procession up the aisle behind our Monarch, a gleaming centrepiece amidst a great orchestra of sound, of pomp and circumstance, against the cathedral backcloth dim and mysterious, so unlike the television setting of a later day. As each part of the long ceremony unfolded, we altered our position according to the dictates of the Earl Marshal, the Duke of Norfolk. Sometimes we sat and I managed to ease my right shoe which, only delivered at five o'clock that very morning, was too short in the toe. After the ceremonies had taken place, we helped the King back into his coach and then piled into a bus to be ready at Buckingham Palace, where, upon arrival, he came under the watchful eye and caring of the Lord Steward, the Duke of Buccleuch, who enquired anxiously whether His Majesty was tired. The King still had to stand for some time in front of photographers before moving out on to the balcony. Then a tumult of faces looked up from below, and a great eruption of sound hit us, a demonstration of the seen and heard power of the Monarchy in Britain. Afterwards all the members of the Royal Family and their Royal guests and members of the Household and we, the Maids and Pages of Honour, sat down to lunch. Princess Juliana, whose make-up was in need of some repair, arrived late and sat at our table. That night we watched the floodlighting and fireworks among the rejoicing crowds.

In October 1937, the beginning of my second year, I was invited by the Ramsdens to keep my horse Hitler at Turweston. As they were to be in Kenya until Christmas and could not ride their horses, I had several beautiful hunters at my disposal. Unfortunately, instead of being able to hunt, I caught bronchitis and was taken to the Ackland Nursing Home where the doctor, suspecting TB, advised me to go abroad. After examining several glossy travel leaflets I chose the Hotel Shelly e Palmes, where I was promised sunshine and palm trees. Before leaving I rode three horses in some hunter trials but felt too weak to put on even a moderate show. I duly went off with a feeling of regret. I was joined at Lerici by Georg Deym. The weather was dreadful and the hotel uncomfortable. I returned to Oxford in time to attend the annual dinner of the Oxford City Branch of the British Legion on St Andrew's night. In my speech I said, "War hangs over us today and it will be our turn next time if war should come. We realize what it means and if the time should come I think there would be as great a response to the call from my generation as there was in 1914."

My friends and I were deeply worried by world events and by the danger of war. We had shared the Nation's anxiety over the result of the Oxford Union debate when the motion 'To refuse to fight for King and Country' had been passed. We listened with dismay to a debate when Liddell Hart spoke against conscription.

Early in 1937, as a member of the Christ Church Canning Club, I listened to an address by Sir Philip Sassoon, Under Secretary of State for Air. He had served as Military Secretary to my father, so after the meeting he came round to my rooms in Tom Quad for a talk. As a result we formed a friendship which was to widen my horizons over the next two years. The following weekend he sent his small aeroplane to take Tony Loughborough and myself to Trent and a number of weekend parties followed, which were great fun, with tennis and golf but with a seriously political atmosphere. Churchill, Eden and Shakes Morrison were among the guests. They were united in their opposition to German policies of aggression and after dinner when the port arrived there were interesting conversations led by Churchill. The atmosphere of Lympne, Philip's other house near Hythe, was less formal than Trent though with beautiful pictures and tapestries. We could enjoy the garden created by our host and sit talking with him and Hannah Gubbay, his cousin. In a moment of great generosity he gave me his car, a splendid Humber Snipe drophead coupe with a Mulliner body, which was to be my prized possession during my time at Oxford. Philip probably owed a lot to my father for his early training. He himself made a valuable contribution to the RAF, visiting and presenting cups to many squadrons all over the country. That year he became Minister of Works, to which office he was suited because of his great taste and knowledge of works of art. He died prematurely on the eve of the war.

My mother had never had a good relationship with Philip, and perhaps for that reason I had missed the chance of knowing him during my early years. My mother alienated some people because of her protectiveness of my father's reputation. Among them was Duff Cooper who wrote the official and excellent biography. My mother felt that, because of his different make-up, Duff Cooper could not understand my father. She, as a Trustee, had been responsible for his appointment and she was ill-advised to go against him. Because he mislaid certain papers, among them a drawing of my father rescuing a wounded Egyptian during the Battle of Atbara, all of which turned up safely but too late to prevent a rift, she decided to do the job herself. Her nights were spent typing the manuscript of her edited edition of the diaries which for her was a labour of love. Although in the end her book was never published, it was printed in proof form and was to be the only edited edition of my father's early pre-war diaries. So in that sense her work was justified. Sadly she must have been lacking in sound advisers who might have helped her to resolve the difficulties with Duff Cooper. In consequence Faber and Faber, who published the Duff Cooper books, advised my mother's co-trustees, Bertie Fisher and my cousin Hugo de Pree, to bring out an interdict against her biography, of which the first volume was already in proof, on the grounds that it would be financially damaging to their publication. So to meet the requirements of the law she scrapped her work and instead wrote another book, *The Man I Knew*, in which no reference to my father's diaries was made. Her views about the choice of sculptor for the Whitehall statue were disregarded and she led the protest against the work of A.F. Hardiman and indeed refused to attend the unveiling ceremony. Hardiman's interpretation, although sculptured in the tradition of Verrochio's statue in Venice, is a symbolic work in a modern idiom which was misunderstood, particularly by cavalrymen who are exact in questions of verisimilitude. This effigy, without a cap, mounted on a horse large enough to carry a rider with boxer-like proportions and with matching hairy heels, was considered to be an insult to the memory of someone whose turnout was immaculate. Among the entries for the competition other quieter and more conventional maquettes for equestrian statues which could be more easily identified had been preferred and many letters of protest had been written to the press. My mother, whose taste in aesthetic matters was never her strong point and, like most widows, preferred to see her husband portrayed in sympathetic and lifelike terms, joined the protesters and decided to absent herself from the unveiling ceremony.

It is possible that the more favourable opinions of Sir Philip Sassoon, who had been Military Secretary to my father and who was now the first Minister of Works, may have saved the project. As soon as the ceremony was over the Secretary of State for War, Leslie Hore Belisha, left his place among the members of the cabinet and came over to Lord Trenchard and myself with an expression of unctuous *schadenfreude* to sound out the views of the father of the Royal Air Force. These were predicatably in line with the thoughts which were going on beneath the top hats in the rows behind me. When the Duke of Gloucester pulled the cord to reveal the statue, the top hats almost stood on end. The Duke was a cavalryman himself and at the four corners of the statue stood two serving and two ex-service members from each of my father's old regiments, the 7th Hussars and the 17th/21st Lancers. Behind them were one hundred old comrades from these two regiments. The setting was as we know it in Whitehall each Remembrance Sunday, with long echoing silences interspersed with occasional words of command or movements of marching men. Among the contingents of regular troops were represented the Navy, the Army and the Royal Air Force, including Indian, Dominion and Colonial detachments. The Officers Training Corps, the Royal Military College and the Royal

Military Academy were also represented. In all some two thousand serving personnel from the Defence Forces were drawn up before the statue. The military parade was completed by some seven hundred members of the Territorial Army. Music was provided by the Metropolitan Police bands.

The general salute on the Duke's arrival was sounded by trumpeters of the Royal Horse Guards (The Blues) of which my father was Colonel and the Guard of Honour was composed of the 1st Battalion Grenadier Guards. After he had unveiled the statue the Duke laid a wreath carried for him by a Metropolitan Police Sergeant who had carried my father's Union Jack pennant with the 17th Lancers escort in France and Flanders. The Duke then gave an address in which he outlined some of the services rendered by my father. Wreaths were than laid by members of his family who included my second sister Doria, who was helped by her eight-year-old son, Douglas, grandson of the Field Marshal. When these ceremonies were over I was proud to have a talk with my father's old Troop Sergeant, then in the mounted police, and with many others who had served with and known him.

Meanwhile my mother continued my father's work for ex-servicemen, of whose needs she was deeply aware. She worked tirelessly for the Poppy Factory she had set up in Edinburgh and she kept constant personal touch with poppy sellers in the big cities around Armistice time. She had what is called the human touch and was extremely popular with all the members of the British Legion and of the Women's Section during her many visits to branches throughout the country. She resolutely followed the Legion motto "Service not Self" to the detriment of her own mental and physical health. In 1938 she made an exhausting journey by air to Australia and New Zealand to visit ex-service organizations. She died the following year.

Back at Oxford I made the most of the pleasures remaining

before the war started. In the winter terms I hunted and in the summer I played polo. During my last year I played in the Oxford polo team which included Philip Profumo and Gavin Astor. We took part in a number of tournaments and in the inter-varsity match at Hurlingham which we won after a hard game in which I scored the winning goal. During my last year I spent less time fox hunting and more time hunting with the drag to which I acted as whipper-in. My main job was Field Master but in spite of my efforts the field usually were in at the 'kill' before the hounds.

During my last season I had two wonderful days hunting in Leicestershire. On each day I was lent two outstanding horses by my host Raymond Greene. On the first day with the Quorn my horse was a grey thoroughbred which had jumped in the Olympic Games at Berlin in 1936. We found in Ragdale Wood and ran straight without a check into the Belvoir Vale where our fox went to ground in Hose Thorns. The distance between the two coverts is nine and a half miles and we covered it at racing pace. We could take our fences as they came without having to stop or to queue. We had another good hunt on the following day with the Cottesmore from Launde Park Wood. We finished up eight miles away near Ashwell Spinney after running for ninety minutes. Unfortunately I stopped for a drink with the Master and his wife on my way home. The drink, called an 'Old Fashioned', was too strong for my tired constitution so that afterwards I found it difficult to make conversation during the dinner party which had been organized and I could hardly get the soup spoon into my mouth. I wrote in my hunting diary: "When Lord Sefton arrived for dinner, I saw two Lord Seftons instead of one."

During my last two years I read for an Honours degree in History but with so many distractions it was difficult to concentrate on the various books required. I enjoyed writing essays for my weekly tutorials, and I found that the dialogue between tutor and undergraduate was a stimulating experience. But although my tutors, of whom the seniors were J.C. Masterman and Noel Myres, were both patient and understanding they felt anxious and uncomfortable. The gap between their standards and my performance was too great. In desperation the Senior Censor tried to stop me hunting by refusing a permit for me to drive my car, but to no purpose. Instead I drove to the meets in cars provided by my friends.

During my last year I succeeded Peter Wood as President of the Bullingdon. We had our own dining room above the Oriel Tea Rooms in Carfax where we lunched each day. During the summer term we held our annual dinner (dressed in blue tail coats with white silk facings) in some neighbouring barn, so as to avoid any damage to the place where we dined. That year Charlie Lansdowne, the Secretary, who was later to be killed in action, and I were anxious to save the annual bill for damage to our bus so we decided to organize a fleet of taxis instead. The bill for damaged taxis was bigger than before; indeed the damage was so great that the Proctors decided to suspend the club, and to impose a fine for which we as Office Bearers were responsible. Happily this incident was not reported in the papers. Sometime before Robin Hastings and I had written a joint letter to the *Daily Telegraph* in which we complained that rebukes for undergraduates' misdeeds were not always well directed. We wrote:

"Whereas our fathers sowed their wild oats in the comparatively secluded company of dons and tutors, our audience is only limited by the circulation of the daily papers. The public gaze is misdirected. The foundations of the Empire are hardly to be shaken by the hail of stones which we are led to believe are directed continually at Belisha beacons. They are, however, threatened by the words and actions of those undergraduates whose principal diversion is to pass treasonable motions."

As things turned out we were wrong. The public gaze was not misdirected, so far as the minor misdeeds of undergraduates were concerned. But our more serious proposal that the affairs of the Union would lead to pacifism and military defeat was also proved unfounded. Perhaps in our hearts we realized that the days of the Empire were numbered. We also knew that our behaviour was not good, but perhaps we excused ourselves on the grounds of "boys will be boys", though the reply might have been *"Noblesse oblige"*. The behaviour of Etonian's, and in my case of Stoics, at Bullingdon dinners, although unpopular with Evelyn Waugh, was a relatively harmless way of letting off steam. However, it might have been an indication that some of us were not taking full advantage of the education which we were privileged to enjoy.

Luckily for me, during my last vacation, which I spent at Bemersyde with Xandra as hostess, Bill McElwee, the Stowe history master, came up to coach me for my final schools, and during a short month's course my friend Gerry Pilkington and I were helped to cover the whole of English history from the time of the coming of the Anglo-Saxons to 1914. I sat the examination in June. Thanks to Bill I was able to pass with a Fourth Class Honours Degree.

My degree, together with the fact that I had served as a member of the Oxford OTC, qualified me for a commission in the Royal Scots Greys. The commission was backdated to January 1938, which gave parity of seniority with those who had passed through Sandhurst.

5

The Middle East

"We'll see our grey horses trample that bugger Hitler into the bowels of the airth." Reservist trooper embarking for service abroad.

In the middle of August 1939 I obeyed War Office instructions to report for duty with the Recruit Training Squadron of The Greys and The Royals at Redford Barracks in Edinburgh. My mess kit was ready ironed for my first night in mess, but instead I went with David Rogers, the second in command, to watch a musical at the King's Theatre and afterwards dined with him and "The Twinnies" who were the leading actresses of the show. Early next morning I settled down to a more orthodox routine of riding school under Sergeant Jenkins when I jumped bareback and did vaulting exercises at the canter. My military experience had been limited to service as a trooper with the cavalry of the Oxford Officer Training Corps and to a month's attachment with the 9th Lancers at Tidworth when I had learnt to maintain and drive light tanks – some of the few available to armoured regiments at that time. As the regiment to which I had now been posted was still mounted on horses I found myself carrying out the same duties that had been laid down for the cavalry by my father during his days at the War Office.

The international situation at this time was critical and war was imminent. In July I had received a farewell letter from my German friend, Georg Deym, telling me that war was inevitable and hoping that we would be alive to see each other again after the war. Hitler was determined to take over the Polish corridor and on the conquest of Danzig on 1 September he bombed Poland. War was declared on 3 September. According to my diary:-

"War declared at 11 o'clock. Soon after there was an air raid alarm. Everyone scuttled to their positions, and the Reservists hurried to the woods as they have no gas masks. In the middle of it all the GOC Scottish Command, Sir Charles Grant, arrived, complete with dogs; so we concluded it was a practice. (In fact it proved to be an enemy attack.) Allotted men to Labour Corps after lunch. The men are going to be used as debarkation workers 'somewhere abroad' and the job is not popular."

"4 September. First parade of the Recruit Training Sqn under Major Handy Hurrell (17th/21st Lancers). Major Sprot came over to try and get his son Aidan into the Regiment.
After lunch the officers dig their own air raid shelters in the cabbage patch.
After tea Michael Lycett, Victor McCalmont and I walked up towards the Pentlands after partridges. With the help of a little poaching – it turned out we were on Bowlby's father-in-law's ground – we bagged a partridge, a rabbit and a pigeon."

The descent of 16,000 Reservists upon a Recruit Squadron of eighty caused some confusion. My task was to detail Reservists for the job of unloading ships, when men naturally wanted to serve with their own Regiments. I allowed them some hopes of joining their Regiments later by letting them understand that the arrangements were only temporary, but very few of them were not to be disappointed. As the men left to join the labour units, the Reservist officers had little to do but stand around talking or digging air raid shelters. Many of them were Masters of Foxhounds and had come straight from cubhunting. Soon the younger ones and those of us who were Regulars were warned for duty abroad and were sent on embarkation leave. I spent some days with the Buccleuchs at Drumlanrig, walking with a gun on the Dumfriesshire hills.

On the last day of my leave I went over to Bemersyde to supervise the preparations for the arrival of eighty blind children from the Edinburgh Blind Asylum. I then returned to Edinburgh and that night left with a large party for an unknown destination with tropical uniform among our kit. We set off at night in lorries with Kid Cator, a veteran from the First War trenches, playing "Tipperary" on his mouth organ. The moon cast shadows on the street as we drove to the station.

Next day at Southampton we went on board the *Franconia* ready in her wartime coat of grey paint for her journey to Haifa. Towards evening we weighed anchor and took a last look at England.

"*28 September/39*. We are in a convoy of 5 liners bound for the East, are escorted by 2 destroyers. We pass seaplanes and hangers all carefully camouflaged. Off Bembridge we stop for some reason. David Rogers sighs when he thinks of the pretty girls he left behind at Bembridge. Dine with David Rogers, Desmond Russell and the Cayzers. Start moving again about 2 a.m."

Next morning I put down my razor and I did not shave my moustache again until after the war. A breeze made white horses on the sea. We spent the morning on deck in the sun reading and at about midday we passed Land's End.

Our convoy consisted of the *Empress of Australia*, the *Alcantara*, the *Athlone Castle* and the *Franconia*, each vessel with an anti-aircraft gun and six-inch gun, sailing in changing formations with destroyers racing up and down like mother ducks nursing their ducklings.

There were days of lolling in deck chairs reading and thinking. Evenings of talking and mild gambling. Those on board were mostly youngish men who were leaving their

This might be a
pleasure cruise except
for the destroyers —

civilian jobs as drafts to almost every unit in the Middle East. There were infantry and cavalry, sappers, gunners, sailors and airmen, members of the Pay Corps and Air Ministry officials. The 11th Hussars stood out in cherry coloured trousers, among them Allenby's son. The reservists comprised civilians from all walks of life and had various backgrounds and make-ups.

Suddenly in the middle of the afternoon of 5 October while I was reading on deck the *Alcantara* charged full bat across our bows. We backwatered frantically but it was too late. There was a great crash in front and all the bows were stove in. Then another crash and I saw the *Alcantara* come crashing against us a few yards from where I was sitting. It looked as if we must sink I picked up my writing things and ran below. Peter Halswell appeared from below looking smug and carrying a small bag prepared for emergencies – whisky, shaving things, pipe tobacco and loo paper. Men with nothing on except life belts (they had been swimming) met me on the companionway. I ran to my lifeboat station where men were quietly assembling without panic. We looked and saw our two lifeboats smashed to smithereens and hoped that no water was coming in. Below us the ship's side was bulging ominously. Evidently our Captain had gone off duty and left the Quartermaster on the bridge, who misread a signal and turned too much to starboard, straight into the *Alcantara*. If we had not had our lifeboats hanging over the edge, which took the bump, we would have almost certainly sunk since we had on board a lot of ammunition. Several men were killed in the bows of the *Alcantara*. The only casualty in our ship was the Captain who fell out of his bunk and broke his collar bone.

Next day we sailed into Valetta harbour as it lay brilliantly lit against the deep blue sky, its ochre stone houses rising in tiers one on top of the other Spanish fashion. Small boats were dashing to and fro. Destroyers were lying at anchor. We were towed into dry dock where our ship was set up on spars, the water let out and we had a chance to examine the damage.

In Malta we enjoyed a peaceful interlude waiting for another ship. Those of us who played polo borrowed Naval ponies for a game on the garrison polo ground. I remember feeling the warm sun in a sailing boat belonging to Charles and Ann Sismey and thinking how lucky we were to be away from the black out and autumn weather at home.

After ten days we were moved from our comfortable quarters in the *Franconia* to a smaller troopship, the *Nevasa*, which took us to Palestine. During the journey, on 18 October, I received a telegram to say my mother was dead. Tired out, she had found rest and peace at last. She was spared the war. During the last years of her life, under the instruction of Father Scanlon, she had been received into the Catholic Church. At her wish she was buried beside my father at Dryburgh. After her death many letters and telegrams of

"Officer on board the Navasa"

condolence from people and organizations at home and abroad reached me in Palestine. I received a kind letter from Walter Buccleuch:

"My dear Dawyck

"We were very pleased you were able to come here for a few days before sailing to join your Regiment, all of us have received your nice letters.

"I am very sorry indeed that you were bereaved so soon after leaving, and hope it is for the best. If only your father had lived a few years longer it would have been a great help to her, and to all of you, and to the Nation, and she would have avoided many of the worries which put such a great strain on a person of her temperament. You have much sympathy from all of us. Your mother was always charming to me and it was very sad that her health was spoilt by too much worry during the last war and the responsibilities left upon her since.

"I make no forecast now about peace but always hear that Halifax expresses optimism. This is a war in which the killing of British, French and German soldiers seems to have very little relation to the objects which we have in view, and I still hope that greater security will be brought to Europe for the future without a process of extermination. A decisive military defeat was necessary in 1918, but I feel differently about it this time and am anxious that prolongation of war too long will bring no glory but sadness and other disasters for all.

"I hope you will have the best luck in the Middle East and will take advantage of every opportunity to get a useful experience in what can be a very interesting part of the world if you are not confined to too small an area. I hope you will get to Egypt, India and many parts of Asia Minor while you are there, and return a very learned person.

"I do not feel like hunting. If more independent I would gladly be back with one of my Regiments, and if things develop after the winter, all will be wanted.

Best of good wishes.
Yours ever
Walter"

My mother's death left me feeling alone and sad. Two days later, when we landed at Haifa, Peter Borwick, the Adjutant, welcomed us in a launch. The air was hot and a khamsin wind was blowing. We reached Rehovot after lunch and were given a warm welcome by the Regiment.

Our men were quartered in long huts and the officers slept in comfortable Jewish houses, empty except for camp equipment. The officers had a verandah where we gathered in white dinner jackets or blue patrols before dinner. Here, soon after our arrival, I came to dine dressed in a smart white dinner jacket made by the Regimental tailor. There was a cool breeze blowing through the bougainvillaea across the verandah and the mess sergeant came up and offered me a drink. Then the sergeant returned without my drink but with a message from the Colonel to come inside. I found the Colonel, pea-green, glowering from an armchair, barking like an angry dog, "Where did you get those shoes?" I looked down at my brown Norwegian slippers polished by my servant Barnes and said they were all I had. "Buy some black

Peter Bowick

ones tomorrow," he growled. I was in too sensitive and low a mood to be able to appreciate his angry tone, and it took me some days to forgive or to understand. Was he being fussy about dress or more likely carrying out a military initiation?

Newly joined subalterns carried out their first duties as orderly officer under instruction. My instructor was Geoffrey Keyes, who was later to win a posthumous VC after a Commando raid on Rommel's HQ. In the course of our rounds we found two soldiers who had been put under arrest in the Guard Room for making some disturbance. The men were demanding permission to fetch their mosquito nets from their huts. Geoffrey granted them permission but also ordered them to be woken up every two hours in order to have Dover cream rubbed on them by the guard.

My contemporaries from Sandhurst were, through their training, more efficient than an Oxford undergraduate and when I took over 4th Troop, B Squadron, I found myself relying on the troop sergeants for guidance and support. In their turn Tarry Shaw, Frank Dodds and Pompey Hunt were all invaluable to me. Sometime later when I inspected the guard as orderly officer I received bad news. Some Australian officers had been causing a drunken disturbance and had been locked in the Guard Room. There was no alternative but to leave them to sleep it off and deal with the diplomatic niceties the following morning.

My arrival coincided with the closing stages of a police-keeping phase when the Regiment was responsible for disarming the Arab marksmen and for supervising the Jews. We cultivated our relations with both the Jews and the Arabs.

I therefore settled down to a routine of troop-training interspersed with police work. The Palestine troubles were, if but temporarily, over and, until the Regiment was mechanized, its main task was to practise tactics and this it could do in a terrain suitable for horses. We looked upon this period as a time of preparation for the mechanization which would enable us to play our part later in the war.

I was in a good squadron under George Trotter, and I was attached to the troop led by Tim Readman and later by Michael Borwick, who both took infinite trouble to teach me the rudiments of troop training.

"*30 October 1939* Squadron training before breakfast. Am now in Michael Borwick's troop. After breakfast I went with Michael and two sections in trucks to try and arrest three men who had robbed an old boy last week at Bashshit near Quatra. We went first to where the men had last been camping but found them gone. Then we found an old man who had his beard tweaked very hard by the Inspector of Police until he gave away his secrets. The men were camping on the hill and their leader had gold in his teeth. We went on in the trucks and then got out in extended formation we advanced on the camp. Several men ran away but we caught about fifteen to start with. Those who had run away were brought back by shots and one of them was one of the wanted men. All the Arabs sat round in a circle being questioned. Then it was found that the other two were away but would come to the police station tomorrow. Then we returned to the trucks with our prisoners. It was very hot. We got back home about 2 a.m."

Our training consisted of mock battles, of practising rear guards and advance guards across country. We camped and bivouacked a good deal under the cork trees. It was a cloudless autumn, settled and warm, until for a few weeks during the winter the weather broke and the ground became a quagmire. Then, borne on high winds, the rain lashed against our tents as we sat around the paraffin lamp analysing our activities of the day. Two or three nights a week we were sent out on police work either mounted or in trucks. Soon after our arrival we drove to cordon and search an Arab village. My diary for 21 October reads:

"About six o'clock I went with Doodle Stanton and James Hanbury to raid a village called Tina about 30 miles south. Two miles short of the village we got out of a truck and split up into two parties of two sections each. Marched in half sections through the dark. Doodle suddenly made us double down a hill and up the other side where we found ourselves in a sort of alley. He kicked open a door where we found about eight Arabs playing cards on the floor. We searched them and their home for arms. One boy was cheeky and Doodle kicked him. We searched another house with a woman giving her child suck; then another with three old women in it. No arms found, though we looked in every nook and cranny – under the eaves, in the water pots, everywhere. The people lay sleeping on the floor, apparently in their day clothes. They grumbled and laughed inwardly at our efforts to discover their arms (which they had got safely hidden). Silently we trudged back down the wadi to our trucks. It had been an interesting evening for me, to see what the Regiment had been doing for the past year, to see what the Arabs and their dwellings are like. I was ticked off by Duggie Stewart for leaving a man's rifle against a wall while the man was searching a roof. 'It won't stay there long,' he said. Some jackals crossed the road as we motored back to Rehovot."

Our enjoyment of the last embers of peace was enhanced by the arrival of several officers' wives who came out from England to set up temporary homes. The general atmosphere of the Regiment became much more civilized as a result; the social activities of lone bachelors were enlivened by occasional dinner parties, picnics to the sea and drives round the Holy Land in battered old Buicks which were sold to us by the Arabs. The wives had abandoned their homes and communities, their horses and dogs, handing over young children temporarily into the hands of others. They found refuge from

As Home from work are go.

Left to right: Lugs Twistleton-Wykeham-Fiennes, Peter Halswell, Peter Borwick, Massey Roborough

the blackouts at home and were able to absorb the emptiness of Palestine wasting time peacefully with their husbands until the time would come for the shooting to begin. The Colonel's wife, Nina, brought out their daughter Caroline who, in partnership with Jane Findlay, daughter of Roland and Ba, were liable to raid our troop lines in search of food for their donkeys. The other camp followers included Jane Roborough, Audrey Fiennes, Joyce Brassey, Mary Readman and Joan Bowlby.

Part of our Troop Leaders' duties consisted of visits to the Muktas of villages where we were entertained under the shade of some fig trees or in the case of richer villages in the comfort of a spacious room. We were offered tea and coffee and orange juice, or on occasion we were invited to a large feast. We all sat cross-legged on carpets or on divans offering compliments to each other in a diplomatic way. One Mukta had served in the Turkish army during the war and said that the English government and justice was much fairer than the Turkish. He said that German propaganda was only in the towns and that, although he did not want to say much about Hitler and European affairs as they wanted to mind their own business, he thought dictatorship rule would be less pleasant than English. Lugs Fiennes said he was sorry if English government was somewhat strict but soldiers had to do as they were told. The Mukta said the Arabs would be quite satisfied so long as no more Jews entered the country. He said there were a few bandits about.

My diary entries for 16 and 17 November, 1939.

"Troop schemes in the morning and return to luncheon. At 7 p.m. our troop rides out in the dusk to do an ambush. On the way a chap (Mitchell just reached 16 years) gets a nasty kick below the knee. Loud moans but a slug out of my flask (his first taste of liquor) puts him up on his feet very quickly.

"Peter [Paget] stops on the main track and I go on with the other half of the troop to another track just over the

Peter Paget

hill. We settle down allotting sentries etc. If anyone comes we pounce, if he runs we shoot. We are waiting for a band of Arabs who are said to be travelling south tonight with a mine they have just manufactured. Anyone passing will be arrested as they will be breaking the curfew. Very cold. Nothing happens.

"Usual afternoon. On one side of the camp the Jews farm the land and are ploughing with modern tractors. On the other a few Arabs are scratching up the ground with an old wooden plough drawn by a camel and a cow, burning the weeds and scrub where they can't even be bothered to scratch."

My diary entry for 30 November and 1 December, 1939.

"England mobilizes a quarter million more men. Either she realises Russia's action will make a lot of the moderate Germans favour peace with England in order to stop the aggrandisement of Russia and she wants to appear strong and to be able to dictate a strong peace or she fears the continuation of combined Russian German action – the conquest of Sweden and Norway and the beginning of a world war.

"Called at 3.30 a.m. Breakfast at 4.00 Drove in trucks to search the village of Junzin near Lydda. The whole Regiment out. A good view from the roof tops of surrounding countryside now rapidly turning green with grass and crops. The people and houses filthy and the inhabitants all looked very ill. Many were blind and one woman could hardly walk as she had a very young baby with black rings round its eyes and her breast was in a terrible state. After our search (several wanted men were found with rifles) we all breakfasted in the square and then drove home. Got a long nice letter from Doria.

My diary described the current situation in Finland.

"The Finns are fighting well though they are badly equipped with material. Tanks etc are old and they are a small army. They have captured forty Russian tanks and have sunk a Russian cruiser from shore batteries. Their commander is good. They have better leaders than the Russians (their leaders having been killed in the Revolution) and they are more used to fighting in the snow. The Russian attacks are severe and the bombing of towns is terrible. By their action it is to be hoped that all neutral countries may take steps towards entering the war and that moderates in Germany may realise the dangers of Russian advance. There was a demonstration in Rome today on behalf of the Finns. On the other hand this may be merely another rung in the Dictatorships' ladder."

The Regiment's involvement in police duties continued. One diary entry read:

"The new law restricting sale of Palestine land to Jews came into force today and there were strikes and demonstrations throughout the country. The police charged the mob in Rehovot and received several bricks in their faces. We turned out after tea to patrol the town. George Trotter very warlike and enjoying it all. Dispersed the mob by the Post office with one shout. Our HQ at the cinema where we are to send patrols from."

Towards the end of December David Callander and I visited the Dead Sea. During our journey back through the

narrow pass my ancient Ford car broke down. We were
breaking the rules in not having an armed escort with us,
driving at night through an area where there were bandits.
Our breakdown took place near the Good Samaritan's Inn
from which we had to walk for about ten miles up the Mount
of Olives to Bethany. This was my first experience of the
reality of the Bible and of the hills of Palestine which gave
new meaning to the Christian instruction which I had
received at home. Christ's teaching, his humility in the face
of God, his suffering and his crucifixion were henceforth to
provide an inspiration which was far greater than when I had
listened to the hollow phrases echoing from the pulpits at
school. I, in my humble capacity as a subaltern in the army
in the early days of a second world war found myself strangely
uplifted as I trudged through the moonlight up the hill to
Bethany, along the road where Christ had passed on his
journey to Jerusalem after spending forty days alone in the
desert. When David and I reached Bethany we were
welcomed by the nuns and David borrowed a bicycle in order
to ride to Jerusalem for some help. Next day my car had been

mended and we reached Galilee to stay with my old friend from Oxford Robin Hastings at Safad.

My diary entry for Wednesday, 20 December 1939 reads:

"Robin took us shooting, not to Lake Hule where there is very good duck shooting because that is now organised by the generals, but we walked down streams and woods leading into the lake. There were a few woodcock about, which we missed, but David shot several black and white kingfishers which seemed rather sad, but you could see him suddenly cheer up as he saw the first bird flutter down. My Arab cartridge-bearer was furious when I refused to fire at a blackbird but Robin explained that the French had been there lately. We had one look into Syria across the frontier and then had to leave for Haifa. It was very nice seeing Robin again. He is evidently doing very well, being Intelligence Officer already and is evidently very good with the Arabs.

"On our way back through Haifa we went to a concert given by the Palestine Symphony Orchestra in which I loved a piece for piano and orchestra by Cesar Franck."

After Christmas 1939 we were joined by Yeomanry Regiments and the Household Cavalry who all arrived in cold weather, their horses having suffered and some of them having died on the journey. We gave up our camp at Rehovot temporarily in order to prepare the camp and horse lines at Latrun for the Sherwood Rangers. We all then formed the 1st Cavalry Division for whom the main diversion was to change camps every three months. In this way we learnt about the country while at the same time enemy spies were being encouraged to think our force was larger than it was.

My diary entry for Wednesday, 13 March, 1940:

"News comes through that Finland has made peace with Russia, much in the latter's favour. Russia receives the

Karelian Isthmus (the door into Finland which Finland defended so well), Lake Ladoga (good base for flying boats), Vipuri, lease of Hengo Island (a good jumping off place to attack Stockholm) and use of the port of Petsamo on the Baltic, and the right of building a railway through Finland to that port and as Finland is limited to small boats in the Baltic Russia gains control there. Thus Russia has got all the strategic points she wants. Finland had offer of a giant expeditionary force from France and England. Why did she refuse it? Because the Scandinavian countries refused to allow us to cross their land because they were frightened of the war spreading to them. Maybe they are only putting off the evil hour or maybe we will be the next to fight."

My diary entry for 24 March 1940 reads:

"Jenin. Our Brigade Commander, late CO of the Regiment, Brigadier Gaisford St Laurence paid a visit.

Touche comes to dinner and expounds his theories of riding which imply that one should ride by balance not grip and lay your thighs across the saddle and sit on them rather than your behind. Then by turning ankles in you get the perfect seat."

My diary entry for 26 March 1940 reads:

"Sent out to clear the sanddunes between Ruben Creek and Jaffa of Bedouins as they are going to build ranges there. We take a tax collector (mounted on a very thin and bedraggled Arab which can hardly raise a walk) with us who values the Arabs land (it only appears to amount to a few stunted fig trees) and we give them twenty-four hours' notice to clear out. I have to do big white man stuff."

The chances of being mechanized in the near future were slim. Most of us felt frustrated. Geoffrey Keyes and Michael Borwick left to join the Commandos and Bill McLean left for Somaliland. In July I was asked by the Colonel, George Todd, to go off and be temporary ADC to General Dick O'Connor commanding the Western Desert Force. This appointment involved me in the war against the Italians. I travelled down to Cairo by train.

My diary entry for Sunday July 28 1940 reads:

"Cairo is very hot and sticky (the beginning of the rains up the Nile) and also very full of soldiers. Very gay after Palestine with a lot of people just up to have three good days' leave and then back to the desert. Dine with Charlie Lansdowne on the roof of the Continental Savoy Hotel. Bed fairly early. Charlie is rather depressed at the war – is not sorry at being turned into searchlights as he does not really like horses 'tho he likes riding them. He says he wouldn't mind being made Italian prisoner as he would get peace?? The war doesn't suit people like Charlie."

I caught the leave train which left Cairo for Mersah Matruh. Along the platform some of the soldiers destined for the operations in the Western Desert were humping their baggage. Compartments were beginning to get jammed up as friends met up with one another. I was bound for duty as ADC to the General commanding the Western Desert Force. Behind my tense expression shone the serenity of an artist detached from the hurly burly and confusion around me. I may have looked confident as I threaded my way through the throng followed by an Egyptian porter carrying my valise. But there were self-doubts as well. I was tall and thin, young looking for my twenty-two years though in some ways mature. My appearance was not altogether impressive. In spite of the regulation moustache and khaki shorts, sunburnt knees and bushshirt my sam browne belt sagged a bit due to my chest and stomach being on the thin side. Leaning from a compartment Robin Hastings, now commanding a company in the Rifle Brigade, saw me appear, hailed me and helped me and my valise into the carriage where several officers including Bill Wainman,

Adjutant of the 11th Hussars, who had been ill with sandfly fever were sitting.

General O'Connor was at the station at Mersah Matruh to meet me and he at once made me feel at home. Small in stature, dressed in shorts, he displayed a personality which was vigorous, intense and deeply serious. Behind the friendly façade lay an expression of grim determination – of vigilance. He seemed like a horse which is eager and almost fretful. His eyes showed something of the deep feelings of his Presbyterian background. On our arrival at Western Desert Force Headquarters at Ma'aten Bagush, I was taken to my tent, which was sandbagged, standing adjacent to the General's. I met Ingolsby, the General's batman, and Simons his driver. Near us was 'A' Mess tent, where I met Brigadier Neil McMicking and other staff officers who seemed to me immensely old – all of them senior officers over fifty years of age. Before dinner the General took me across the dunes to the sea, where we left our towels and swam naked. Many long and tiring days of desert journeys were ended with this cool form of recreation, and often as we drove through the sand and heat we looked forward to the evening bathe, which became a ritual for all the soldiers, friend and foe alike, along the seashore.

The Italians were along the frontier between Libya and Egypt which we were guarding. They were preparing to advance. It was very interesting to see how military formations operated on the ground; how the ambulance and the ordnance and the Army Service Corps actually worked; how the single road was used; how the railway was used. Instructions and visits took place most days. The ADC had to plan visits ahead. He had to work the sun compass and chart the desert journeys from one unit to the next. He had to fix up with units what time and when we would get to them on a tour of inspection. He had to make sure that the route was going to be fairly safe, that there were no minefields on the way (our own minefields). There was a day when we had been misinformed about a minefield and we went slap down the middle of it. I was with the General in the front car, the batman coming on behind, and suddenly there was a frightful explosion and the car behind blew up and with it the General's driver and batman. We pulled them out and they were pretty black and blue but they weren't seriously wounded. It was a rather nasty experience and I am glad to say I was exonerated from all responsibility because we had not been informed of the existence of the minefield.

The General was without any small talk, he spoke with temperament often tinged with anxiety and frustration. To be alone with such a man for hours on end driving through the desert was not going to be easy. Anybody who knew him had an enormous regard for him. They would have done anything for him. He was a selfless man. I think he was a

Brigadier Strafer Gott looks down on General Dick O'Connor

wonderful leader and it was a great tragedy that he was put in the bag in 1941. He was totally without any sort of side or ambition. He was thoughtful for others. He was a deep-thinking man, very quiet and introvert. He was completely absorbed in the task at hand. His closest confidant was the Commander-in-Chief, General Wavell, whose opinions were sacrosanct. He paid regular visits to General Dickie Creagh who commanded the 7th Armoured Division, The Desert Rats, which comprised two armoured brigades and the support group under Brigadier Strafer Gott. Armoured cars of the 11th Hussars provided a reconnaissance screen sending out patrols ready to give early warning of movements by the enemy.

Our C-in-C was at that time at home in Britain in order to urge the Government to send him more troops and equipment, guns and tanks. The Prime Minister was deeply aware of the dangers in the Mediterranean and of what might happen if the enemy pressed an all out attack on the Nile simultaneous with a landing in Britain. He therefore called for an armoured brigade to be rushed by fast convoy through the Mediterranean to fill the breach. Wavell supported the more cautious views expressed by the general staff about the route and the brigade was despatched on the understanding that it would be routed round the Cape unless the desert situation became critical. The moment for decision would be left until around 26 August when the convoy reached Gibraltar.

At night, lying awake in my tent at Ma'aten Bagush the only sound was of an occasional Italian bomber on its way to Alexandria or Cairo. Air activity was relatively light on both sides, although a number of thermos and other bombs were being dropped around our camp. From our side the Air Force was trying to prevent the build up of enemy force and supplies. Swordfish of the Fleet Air Arm assisted a small RAF force of Lysanders and Gladiators. The Navy based

The Night RAIDER.

on Alexandria with an inadequate number of ships was trying to keep our sea route through the Mediterranean open and free of danger from lurking enemy submarines and at the same time her destroyers were helping the ground forces from the sea. Patrols of the Long Range Desert Group were getting ready to bring harassment behind the lines of the enemy.

Behind our lines lay a network of supplies of water and food, ammunition and petrol placed in dumps separated and camouflaged because of danger from the air. Our railhead was at Matruh, whence hospital trains transferred the wounded back to field hospitals at Daba or to the base hospitals in Alexandria and Cairo. The casualties, apart from those caused by wounds, were mainly cases of dysentery, sandfly fever and desert sores.

The day after my arrival we drove about 250 kilometres across the desert to 7th Armoured Brigade Headquarters on the Libyan frontier. We travelled in two cars. The General's car in front flying a red pennant was usually driven by himself or by me. Sometimes we transferred to the second car if our own car broke down because of overheating or a puncture. On our way we inspected recovery detachments and field ambulances. On the following day we visited the 11th Hussars where someone gave me my first glimpse of the enemy – small specks through the shimmering mirage. The enemy was too far away to make the experience a very meaningful one. We visited detachments of the RHA and a squadron of the 6th RTR and a company of the 2nd Rifle Brigade. We then

walked down the Halfaya Pass, leaving the cars because the road had been mined for an enemy advance. Having rejoined our cars we drove to spend the night with the 1st KRRC where I found my cousin George de Pree. Next day, after a conference with General Creagh and Brigadier Gott at 7th Armoured Division Headquarters, we drove back home to our Headquarters, inspecting line-of-communication formations on the way. Next day it was the ambulance train's turn to be inspected. The compartments were found to be dirty, the blankets were not disinfected and men were still in their boots. (All these deficiencies had been put right when the

train was inspected a few days later.) The General next spent some time examining the siting of anti-tank mines and hedgehogs in the defences at Mersah Matruh, at Naghamish and at Daba. These could be important rear defences in the event of an enemy breakthrough. My diary entry for 9th August showed that we wanted to deprive the enemy of water and to force him back into the desert where there were no wells.

My diary entry for 13 August 1940 reads:

"Drove in to Alexandria starting 7.30 arriving 11.15. Met the General at his hotel and went with him to lunch on board HMS *Warspite* with Admiral Cunningham who talked to me about the Borders as he comes from Edinburgh. Rear Admiral Willis (Chief of Staff) and Rear Admiral Renouf also there.

My grandmother, née Rachel Veitch of Bawyck, wife of John Haig, owner of the Haig distilleries.

2. My mother, Dorothy Vivian, c.1903. Her "harum-scarum nature was part of her attraction for my father" (p.6).

My father as a subaltern in the 7th Hussars, 1886.

4. My father in 1887.

5. My sisters Doria and Xandra, with their Sealyham terrier Peter, at Eastcott, Kingston Hill, c. 1921 (see p.10)

6. My sister Rene and I in 1924

7. My father and myself with Miss Watson, 1928.

8. My father on a visit to the Poppy Factory at Richmond on the day he died. On the right is Major Howson, the Manager. The Factory still exists, but with more modern equipment.

9. My father's funeral, 1928. The cortege passing the Cenotaph (see p.26).

10. "Great Uncle Walter... was proud of Aunt Violet who kept house for him" (p.40).

Uncle Walter.

Aunt Violet.

'My mother chose Cargilfield near Edinburgh" (p.31). Myself at prep school, 1929.

12. At the unveiling of the memorial at Thiepval. 1932 (see p.38).

13. With my mother, 1935.

14. As a page at the Coronation of HM King George VI, 1937. I am on the King's right (see p.49).

15. With the Royal Family on the balcony of Buckingham Palace after the Coronation. I am on the extreme right.

16. Hunting with the Bicester, 1938. On the left is Tom Egerton.

17 Oxford Hunter Trials, 1938.

18. Bullingdon Club, Oxford, 1939. *Standing l. to r.*: Gavin Astor, Ian Farquhar, Viscount Ednam, P.B. Fielden, R.G. Kison, R.A. Simpson; *seated centre*: A.M. Lyle, Hon R.M. Berry, P. Profumo, E.P. Marsden; *seated front*: E.L.N. Sturt, Marquess of Lansdowne, Earl Haig, G.H.L. Pilkington, F.F.G. Heathcoat-Amory.

Excellent lunch. Returned in Admiral's barge and went on to aerodrome where the General saw General Creagh who is on his way to Cairo.

"Saw 'Follow the Fleet' (Fred Astaire and Ginger Rogers) and stayed night at Windsor Hotel."

I should have added that when we were piped into the Admiral's barge and ferried back to land, we were only to find to my embarrassment that I had forgotten to lay on a car. There was nothing for it but to set off on foot in the terrific heat back to the hotel in Alexandria. The General was not pleased but forgiving.

On 3 September the Commander-in-Chief arrived by air accompanied by General Jumbo Wilson, GOC-in-C BTE and Major General Arthur Smith, Wavell's Chief of Staff. Together with General Creagh our party went round the defences at Naghamish Nullar and Matruh. In their discussions the Generals believed that an Italian attack in the desert was imminent, and that it might well coincide with a landing in Britain. If an invasion was to take place it would probably happen at once in order to avoid the time of the equinoctial gales. Such an attack would really need the help of the Germans if it was to succeed, but it was doubtful whether landings would be possible in the small harbours. It would take time before the Germans would become acclimatized to the desert, so they would be unlikely to be ready to take part in any immediate Italian attack. Next day on 4 September the General showed General Beresford Pierce, commanding 4th Indian Division, and his staff the line which they would defend along the Naghamish Nullar. Each battalion would hold 2,000 yards.

My diary entry for 9 September reads:

"On leave in Cairo. Visit Peter Stirling in Embassy and shop in morning. Francis Fisher comes to lunch. We have a long talk. I then drive down to Alex to the Windsor Hotel. Sunset over the Fleet as we pass. Activity on the Front today. An Italian Division has moved up opposite Sidi Omar."

On 9 September the Italians moved a division up to the frontier near Sidi Omar. On Friday the 13th they crossed the wire in three columns, supported by dive bombers and moved cautiously down the Halfaya Pass to Sollum.

My diary entry for 13 September reads:

"Italians have got into Sollum and are advancing across the wire with one division helped by dive bombers in three columns one just west of Halfaya stretching back to Musaid with armoured cars, medium tanks and guns – one head Bir Sleman – one head PT 207 518364. The small amount of MT behind indicates no great movement. Bombs fell within two miles of us last night in Sidi Hamish area."

By 15 September they had reached a line five kilometres west of Buqbuq. Our troops, the 1st KRRC and Coldstream Guards, retired back to Sidi Barrani, whilst the 1st RTR, the 2nd RB and the 11th Hussars kept level with the enemy along the escarpment to the south, supported by gunners who, with their 25 pounders, inflicted heavy casualties on the enemy. The hot khamsin wind helped to slow up the enemy's advance. After the Italians had reached Sidi Barrani, a derelict spot, on the evening of 16 September, the Italian papers proclaimed it as a place where the trams were already running. Here their drive into Egypt halted and their men began to dig trenches behind barbed wire. As the tanks of the 7th Armoured Division were now needing maintenance, they were brought back to Khulda, while the support group, together with the 11th Hussars, were left to hold a line running south-west from Matruh. My diary entry for 16 September reads:

"The General does not consider this a real invasion, as there is no great army coming up from behind, and he thinks it is only a blind for a greater Italian attack in the Sudan."

On 19 September General Wavell flew down to visit the front line. During the flight, according to his ADC, Francis Fisher, the son of my guardian, the General had written a chapter of his book on Allenby. Next day my General flew off to Siwa to examine the situation there, in case the Italians were to attack south of the Qattara Depression, and on the following day he inspected the defence position of 16th Infantry Brigade at Naghamish, where pillboxes roofed with cement were sited just behind crests to surprise the enemy.

The situation was now stable and the danger of a major Italian attack was over. Our forces lay watching from behind the Matruh line. Preparation of the defensive boxes further behind at Naghamish and near Bagush were busily in hand. Reinforcements were coming down from Palestine and a convoy carrying an armoured brigade was on its way from home. In his despatch dated 10 December 1940 Wavell described the events of this small battle: "The withdrawal of our small force was effected with admirable skill, and there is no doubt by the artillery which was boldly and effectively handled, and whenever opportunity offered by machine gun and small arms fire. Our own losses were under 50 men and a small number of vehicles." My General began to relax or perhaps I should say his mind became less burdened and for short periods he was able to forget his military problems. Sometimes we had talks about hunting and point-to-points before the war. Being free to concentrate his attention on lesser things, he instructed the mess waiters to wage constant warfare upon the flies. His mind also focused on our meals. When he brought back some asparagus from Cairo, with strict instructions to see the long stalks were left on and served with butter sauce, his orders fell on deaf ears and the asparagus was

H.H. Prince Ismael Daoud

served butterless and nearly stalkless in the middle of a large dish. The Egyptians gave us some lighthearted diversion.

Sometimes we called on their units on our way to the front line. Their commander, HH Prince Ismael Daoud, was a Turkish prince, tall, fair and dashing, with an eyeglass, blue cavalry cap and chain mail on his shoulders. His girth indicated the standard of the food in his mess and he was liable to greet us with the words, "Come in and have a bucket of gin".

Our tours of the front line and of the lines of communication continued. Many long and tiring days of desert journeys ended with an evening swim and often, as we drove through the sand and heat, we looked forward to the evening bathe which became a ritual for all the soldiers, friend and foe alike, along the seashore. Further south was an area of harder desert land which stretched between the coast and the Qattara Depression and where vehicles would not get stuck in the sand. To the immediate eye the ground seemed flat, but actually was full of escarpments, of small undulations and hillocks which were of tactical importance. In the evening when the sun was low the desert, with its far horizons and scrubby vegetation, became strangely beautiful. The beauty of the evening light was accompanied by a cool breeze, and when we spent nights on our desert rounds we woke in the morning with our sleeping bags damp in the dew.

In early October Eden arrived at Alexandria and came to stay at our Headquarters. 'A' Mess became heavy with top brass and I was kept busy organizing cars and aeroplanes and rendezvous. The purpose of Eden's mission was to examine the situation on the ground and to make sure that every effort was being made both to defend the Nile and to plan an attack against the enemy. How fruitful those plans would be no one then quite knew. The great successes which would occur in December were beyond our hopes.

At the end of October my time as temporary ADC came to an end. Sadly I said goodbye to General O'Connor and drove off back to Cairo.

I rejoined my Regiment at the beginning of November 1940. I found it beside the Mediterranean at Acre, having come there via Tiberias from Beisan where I had left it in July.

A short time later the Regiment moved over the mountains and down the other side to Jericho in the Jordan valley. Our journey took three days of march. As we rode down the Jordan, stopping on our way to let the horses drink and cool themselves in the river, our Squadron Sergeant Major Bathgate, a dour Scot, filled a bottle to send home for his baby's christening in Edinburgh Castle. It was almost a recreation to be able to ride through this lovely landscape of orange groves interspersed with sandy pastures and cactus hedges after my time in the stifling desert without exercise and with only motor vehicles and dumps of materials to catch the eye.

John Warrender (now Lord Bruntisfield) describes an incident on that march:

"Amongst my brother officers when I joined the Regiment in Palestine in 1940 was Alastair, Earl of Macduff, son of

Prince Arthur of Connaught who had been Colonel-in-Chief of the Regiment. Alastair had been in the Regiment for some seven years and even when I joined had yet to be considered adequate to command a troop. A charming, good-looking man, he had been massaged in and out of Sandhurst and was of very little intelligence. He would never, had he not been his father's son, have been accepted by the Army, let alone by the Royal Scots Greys. He was actually a sad and bewildered man, totally incapable of playing the role thrust upon him, however hard he tried, and he really did try too. However in the eyes of my fellow subalterns and I, with all the heartlessness of youth, he was a glorious figure of fun and the source of hilarious entertainment.

"What follows is but one incident that occurred. In the autumn of 1940, or thereabouts, the Regiment moved from Acre to Jericho – a distance of perhaps 70 miles and a three-day journey. Riding along at the head of 38 men and 40 horses I felt immense pride passing through the Plain of Esdraelon towards the Jordan valley, over the foot hills of Carmel, through olive groves and orange groves, along roads, down goat tracks and along the rocky hills of Palestine. It was a joy to be nineteen years old and an officer in what I believed then, and still believe now 60 years on, to be the finest regiment in the British Army. We halted that evening in an olive grove where we were to spend the night. The horses were picketed and tied in lines made from ropes and stakes carried by each soldier on his horse. There they were groomed, fed and watered, as too, later, were our men and ourselves. The men slept in the open beside their horses and a few small tents were put up for the officers, in one of which was Humphrey Guinness, our Squadron Leader, and Alastair, each of whom wore false teeth. Humphrey removed his as he went to bed and placed them in a glass of water on his camp table, adding some Milton to the water, whilst Alastair, getting into his blankets merely placed his on the table. Both went to sleep. Later Alastair awoke and reached out for a glass of water. Picking up Humphrey's glass he drank a mouthful of the Milton mixture and in disgust threw the contents out of the tent into the olive grove. Of course out went Humphrey's teeth as well. Come the morning Humphrey woke up, still somewhat bemused from the previous night's nightcap of whisky and seeing a set of teeth on the table picked them up and, thinking they were his, even though he was puzzled that they were not in Milton, put them in his mouth and went off to breakfast. Alastair, as was his wont, slept on, dressing in a rush at the last moment, searched wildly for his teeth, obviously without finding them, and went off to have his breakfast. Whilst Humphrey was struggling with his eggs and bacon and wondering why his teeth unexpectedly seemed so uncomfortable, in walked a toothless Alastair who apologized to Humphrey for his late appearance explaining that he had lost and couldn't find his teeth. The awful truth of what had happened suddenly dawned on Humphrey who, spitting out Alastair's teeth with a mouthful of scrambled eggs, rose in his wrath. Alastair, by now thoroughly alarmed, flew out into the olive grove and in his flight stepped on Humphrey's teeth lying there in the dust, crushing them irreparably. You can imagine what then ensued and the joy with which my fellow subalterns reacted."

Our camp had a good prospect near the Dead Sea. We were surrounded by hills without much vegetation. This was where Christ spent his forty days of meditation and the area where the Dead Sea Scrolls were discovered. Riding about on troop training was like riding about on the moon; we were haunted by an eerie feeling of desolation.

The first morning after our arrival at Jericho as the Reveille trumpet blew my tent fell down, a strange reminder of the happenings in the Bible. A few days later I was able to give a talk about my experiences in the Desert and the exploits of General O'Connor.

John Warrender describes another incident:

"One day, whilst we were stationed in Jericho, Dawyck and I were invited to have Sunday lunch with the High Commissioner, Sir Harold MacMichael and Lady MacMichael at Government House in Jerusalem. Also invited was our commanding officer, George Todd. Originally a Gunner, then a 9th Lancer, he had finally transferred to the Greys to command. He had never really been accepted by the senior Greys officers as one of them, though to us young officers he was the Colonel and we had no feelings about his past history. However, we did see him to be rather more interested and concerned with our turnout and smartness than he was in our potential belligerent attitudes and attainments. In particular he had a fixation about the length of our hair. Dawyck and I were delighted therefore when during the course of this somewhat intimidating lunch party we overheard Lady MacMichael say to the Colonel, next to whom she was sitting, and whilst she glanced at us two. "George – what I really like about your officers is that they turn themselves out to look like gentlemen and they don't go in for that horrible short back and sides business like so many others do nowadays in the Army." A sickening silence fell upon the Colonel. Dawyck and I could have kissed Lady MacMichael."

At that time the backs of the horses in my troop became affected by boils and lumps and, on the advice of the vet, I bathed them with disinfectant and hot water. Unfortunately I used my shaving kettle so that germs were transferred from the horses to my chin and before long I too suffered from boils and lumps. I could not shave and was put in hospital in Jerusalem. In spite of the attention from army skin specialists of the best Harley Street variety, no cure could be found. I met

Roland Findlay in the streets of Jerusalem while out walking from the hospital. In his own vein of facetious wit he remarked, "My God, here comes Jesus Christ in person". As officers were not allowed beards I was sent off on sick leave for Christmas accompanied by Bill Maclean and Alastair Macduff to Luxor where we joined up with Sir Miles Lampson's party from Cairo. Jacqueline Lampson, the British Ambassador's young wife, and Freya Stark were among the party. We had a very interesting time touring the temples and tombs on donkeys by day and in the evening had a gay time in paper hats. On the advice of the Ambassador I consulted the local Egyptian doctor, who, after a course of three injections, killed my germs and restored my face to normal.

The Regiment was doing its best to preserve its morale in a situation where it was in limbo and out of touch with the realities of war. But decisions were being taken in the corridors of power which would have a decisive effect upon our future. The Prime Minister was focusing his mind on the problems in the Middle East and detailed instructions were reaching Wavell about how to ward off the invading Italians. From his past experience as a subaltern in the 4th Hussars, Churchill thought about the cavalry and in particular about the future of the three regular cavalry units, the Household Cavalry, the Greys and the Royals. On 8 September he addressed a memorandum to the Secretary of State for War and to the Chief of The Imperial General Staff:

"It has been heartbreaking for me to watch these splendid Units fooled away for a whole year. The sooner they form armoured units the better. Please let nothing stand in the way. It is an insult to the Scots Greys and the Household Cavalry to tether them to their horses at the present time. These historic regiments have a right to play a man's part in the war. I hope to see your telegram approving this course of action before it goes."

It took some time for this instruction to filter through and it was not until Christmas that our Colonel was able to tell the Regiment assembled round the boxing ring at Jericho that we would be mechanized. As he put it:

The cheers that greeted the announcement could almost have been heard over the Judaean Hills in Jerusalem."

Hugh Brassey, then a Captain in the Regiment, wrote the following poem describing an exercise which took place early in 1941 between C Squadron, commanded by Massey Roborough, and B Squadron, commanded by Humphrey Guinness. "The Dear Old Thing" was James Hanbury. The Colonel was George Todd. I was "in the lead" of B Squadron.

A SCHEME – JERICHO 1940
A scheme was made, and a plot was hatched,
The same old scheme, but a bit more patched.
A Military Contest, closely matched,
And us from slumber rudely snatched.
We read the scheme with pity and pain,
What! Massey and Humphrey at war again?
We thought by now it was fairly plain,
These schemes were things made up in vain.

Massey a brigand, a nasty old man,
At Kafr al Fauqua, bunching his plan,
Humphrey to slaughter him – if he can,
Thus the situation when the scheme began.

Humphrey hid the squadron well out of sight,
Sent out patrols and sat back tight.
Said he, "I'm damned if I'm going to fight.
Till I make sure that it's quite all right."

Massey's plan was to hold out a bait,
By offering the Dear Old Thing on a plate,

When Humphrey attacked him, he would wait,
Then bite him in the botty and seal his fate.

So they both sat back and nothing occurred.
The Patrols never sent back a single word.
By the lunchtime hour not a thing had stirred,
And it looked as though the battle would be much deferred.

The Colonel arrived – as an Arab – at the trot,
No spika Engleesh, and that sort of rot,
Massey's still drinking, the dirty old sot,
Attack him now, and You've got him at the pot.

Humphrey heard the news in great elation,
Recalled his troops from their various stations,
Having sent them out on false information,
Off he set to retrieve the situation.

So off they cracked and the pace was fast,
They staggered down a Wadi and a horse got cast,
A lost leading pointer galloped past
Cannoned into Humphrey, and quaked at the blast.

On they went with Dawyck in the lead,
Most of his troop had lost their feed.
He shouted orders, but there wasn't any need,
For they went too fast to pay any heed.

Up the Wadi Auja like birds on the wing,
Round Kafr at Fauqua they formed a ring,
When suddenly a rifle went off. – Ping!
The way was blocked by the Dear Old Thing.

They attacked him left, they attacked him right,
They forced the poor old thing to fight,
But when they had him in terrible plight,
He leapt on his horse and retired from sight.

Humphrey retired for a well-earned rest,
He went up a hill and he sat on the crest.
He'd won the battle, and worked his best,
Away with worry and military zest.

And so his Squadron hacked off back,
Took out their lunch from their haversack.
The Umpires sniggered at things so slack,
And waited for Massey's counter-attack.

They knew that Humphrey was properly caught.
If only Massey did what he ought.
But Massey's attack came all to nought,
It was launched all right – but two miles short!

So Humphrey thought he'd had a good crack,
Girthed up his horses and hacked off back.
Leaving Massey seven miles back,
Awaiting news of his counter attack!

Early in the New Year the Regiment moved from Jericho
to Jenin. On the way we fought a mock battle against an
infantry battalion. Then at the end of April Hugh Brassey,
the gunnery officer, Duggie Stewart, the signals officer, and
I, the driving and maintenance officer, were all sent to Cairo
on courses in order that we might learn the technical intri-
cacies of our new concerns. My D and M course consisted
mainly of the theory of the workings of the internal combustion engine. My memories are of drawing a lot of diagrams
of the insides of engines in variegated colours. We were also
carefully schooled in the best way to give lectures and how
not to play with the chalk while doing so. From the practical
point of view the course was of no great help. When it came
to mending the engine I was useless. I felt out of my depth,
particularly over tank maintenance. After about 75 hours'
running, the aero engines of the Honey tanks had to be lifted

out by means of a chain attached to some metal ring protruding from the garage wall. The chain in turn attached to the engine by means of wire. The whole thing was somewhat home made and we were none of us experts. Unfortunately the wire slipped on one occasion and the engine fell a foot or so on to the concrete and was badly cracked. This was a great tragedy because Honey tanks were very scarce at that time in the Middle East. Luckily a court of inquiry was avoided and our ordnance officer (REME was not yet in being) was held responsible for the accident, and my responsibility for the tanks was limited to the time when they were "on the road".

My diary entries for 26 and 29 May read:

"Am sent with twelve men to receive the Australian Division which is on its way from Matruh to the north. Arrived at Benyamina station last night to make arrangements. Am woken up at 5.30 am to find an Australian Brigadier bending over me asking about his troops. The first party, about 700, arrived by train at midday and are parked in orange groves and given food. I have to also meet their road party and look after that and tomorrow morning I have to send the whole party off to Affule (the concentration area) having packed the train party into Reserve MT. It is all very hard work, especially as trains and convoys are never on time. Bunny Cayzer and Willie Ransome are helping me. I have nine cooks who work very well. We also have to fill up all MT with petrol and oil and see it's properly dispersed.

"Today we have the hardest work of the lot. Brigade have no transport to collect our surplus supplies so we have to do the lot ourselves. Finally having parked the petrol at Benyamina station and the utensils in the train we start off for Haifa with two lorries piled high up like pictures you see of refugees in Flanders. We have no brakes and nearly run into several trucks – a frightening feeling advancing at 2 mph at an object 100 yards off knowing you can't stop and that your load will cause a good impact! We drop our stores at Haifa and just make the dark back to Jenin after four very hard days work."

At this time the Germans were arriving in North Africa. On 5 June 1941 I wrote in my diary:

"Matters are coming to a head in Syria. If we go in now we should just get there before the Germans have time to land many troops by air and sea. We should be justified in doing so because the French are allowing German airplanes to land there. By doing so we would not only prevent the enemy gaining a foothold in Syria but we would also secure a line of communication through Turkey, which we hope may one day become a base for attacking operations northwards and westwards into Europe."

About 12 June a small force called TODCOL commanded by Colonel Todd – consisting of two squadrons (1 Greys and 1 Staffs) with a Greys HQ squadron – set off for Syria as part of the invasion forces. Mounted in old 15-cwt Transjordan Frontier Force trucks, they took part in some tough fighting in the hills near Mir Jayoum. The Greys squadron under Roland Findlay was attacked by a French infantry brigade supported by tanks and guns and was partially surrounded. Under the support of the Australian Bofors guns which knocked out eight French tanks, they were able to retire to a better position. A few days later on 27 June Peter Halswell and I went up to visit TODCOL, which was then in reserve. We found them in a quiet gorge of the River Litani just south of Mir Jayoum. I enjoyed the beauty of the landscape but, as my diary records:

"Only when I stopped to look more closely did I perceive the less pleasant details – every few yards a piece of 75 shrapnel, or a bomb crater. No sign of life except for the soldiers sitting round in tin hats looking rather bored. Animals lying around were dead. 9 cows were luckily lying 100 yards downwind of the RHQ, killed a week before. The church and the farm buildings were full of holes. Many trees were riddled by machine-gun bullets and shorn of their leaves; an extraordinary mixture of peace and quiet with horrors of war. Just up the road a troop of 25 pounders were firing all they were worth on to the far side of Mir Jayoum."

During this time the remainder of the Regiment at Jenin went on with its preparation for mechanization, and to speed things up I used officers' cars, some of whose owners were in Syria, to start driving lessons. I was not popular when their owners returned. We also acted as "hosts" to eight Vichy officers who were virtually prisoners of war. Here is my impression of them in my diary for 29 June:

"I took our French 'guests' into Haifa for a bathe. There are staying with us now the Deputy High Commissioner for Syria, his Chief of Staff (a very nice colonel of Spahis), his ADC and several military policemen from Damascus. They all seem to be anti-Hitler. They felt France was unprepared at the beginning of the war and had to pack in. They admit they allowed Germans to land aeroplanes in Syria, and one feels they might not have resisted so stiffly had the Free French not attacked them. In their words, 'A fight between two brothers or between people of the same nation is always worse'."

After the Syrian campaign ended, the Regiment was reunited. The horses were handed in after the last and farewell Grey Horse Race took place near Sarafand. We were given Honey tanks and mechanized training took place in earnest.

My task was to supervise the driving lessons on the road which took place mostly in trucks. I was responsible for the teaching of tank driving and for lectures on the working of the internal combustion engine. I believe my lectures on that subject were liable to encourage sleep on the part of my listeners.

John Warrender describes them:

"The Army used to have, and doubtless still does have, an ability almost an obsession to place square pegs in round holes. It was therefore no surprise to find, when we were mechanized and our horses removed, that Dawyck Haig had been chosen to go on a course to learn about internal combustion engines whence he could come back to the Regiment and teach all the rest of us how to manage in our new role. He was to teach 400 Scots Greys how to drive, how to look after our vehicles, how they worked and what we were to do when they did not work. Dawyck in the eyes of the Army was the ideal officer for this job. After all he was old enough to have had a driving licence before the war and had even owned a car in peacetime. Furthermore he was the epitome of a cavalry officer, a fine horseman with a good leg for a boot and perhaps the least mechanically minded of all of us subalterns. These qualifications, in the Colonel's eyes, made him tailormade for this appointment. So off he went to some mechanical school and after a very few weeks back he came to the Regiment with an armful of training manuals. He immediately set to work and drew up extensive programmes of courses for senior officers, for junior officers, for non-commissioned officers and for troopers. Each and all of us were to go back to school. So on the due day I turned up with my brother junior officers, each of us armed with a pencil and copious note book at the class room allocated to us, and awaited our teacher. In came Dawyck and began to draw on the blackboard. He was then already a considerable artist but what he drew beyond having a strong phallic appearance looked like nothing any of us had ever seen before. When he stood back to look at this work of art, however, he seemed satisfied, so picking up his swagger cane, and using it as a pointer, he began. I should at this stage explain that what he had drawn was a piston inside a cylinder. 'Now this bit,' he began, pointing to the piston, 'goes up and down inside that bit,' pointing to the cylinder. 'You just first of all of course switch on the engine. Then when it goes down it sucks in petrol. Then it goes up again and it squashes the petrol. Then it sets fire to it and there's an explosion. Down that bit goes again and then it comes up again and drives out all the smoke and the gases. And that's what turns the car's wheels round and makes the car go. It sounds rather complicated but its really quite simple. Just remember suck – squeeze – bang – banish. That's all there is to it. Any questions?' One of our more mechanically minded officers at this point asks brightly, 'How do you stop the thing when you don't want it to suck, squeeze, bang and banish any more?' 'You turn the key off of course,' says Dawyck. 'I don't quite understand this sucking and squeezing and banging and banishing business,' asks another. 'How on earth does that make the wheels go round?' Dawyck searches frantically in his manual, to no avail. 'That,' at last he says brightly 'will be the subject of our next lesson.'

Lessons on similar lines developed over the following few days until at last we were considered competent enough to take and drive the one and only Honey tank at that time on the strength of the Regiment. It was enormous fun. We drove furiously about the Plain of Jezreel just as 3,000 years ago Jehu had done in that very place, raising clouds of dust. We were amazed at our new-found skills and of course murmured to ourselves, which gave us confidence, those magic words Suck Squeeze Bang Banish. Occasionally during the years of war which followed, this magic formula became almost a prayer to me in moments of fear and of stress. Even today, sixty years on, as I sit in a traffic jam the words come back as I listen to the engine ticking over. But still today, should an engine suddenly fail to suck, squeeze, bang and banish and I have looked at the gauge and find that there is still petrol in the tank, I have no idea what on earth to do. Just as once I had to ask on the wireless for help from the LAD, now I have to ring for the AA on a mobile telephone. '*Tout ça change, tout c'est la même chose*', as is also my love and friendship for my dear old brother officer and instructor!"

With our few tanks we practised moving in formation across the growing barley fields and learning to use the wireless sets which enabled troop officers to communicate with their tanks and with their squadron leader.

To keep us smart Colonel George Todd put the Regiment back "on the square" for drill parades and to keep us fit we were made to run each morning before breakfast. Curiously the Colonel appointed me Football Officer, a game which I had always hated, but which enabled me to cheer on the Regimental side during its matches.

Early in March 1942 I was invited by Gerald Grosvenor, Brigade Major of 1st Armoured Brigade, to become his GSo3. His Brigade, which had fought in Greece, had now been re-equipped with tanks and was training in the Delta. Having agreed to go on the understanding that I could rejoin my Regiment after a few months, I departed, leaving my horse Birdcatcher which had been retained with a few others for recreational purposes in the hands of John Warrender. I duly arrived at a tented camp near Mena. Then at the beginning of May, after a few weeks' training, we were sent up to the desert to arrive in the middle of what was later to be known as the 'Cauldron' battle, ready, as we hoped, to be used in a 'knockout' blow on Rommel, who had become encircled by our tanks and was unable to get his supplies through the minefields at his back. We were fresh, we had trained as a unit for many months, fully equipped and ready for battle. When we arrived to the rear of 8th Army HQ a terrible khamsin wind blew up and enveloped us in sand. Brigade HQ was full of anticipation and tension. Our Intelligence Officer was sent off to Army HQ in order to find out the latest situation and to collect a gold pencil which the Brigadier had left at the HQ the day before. Meanwhile Brigadier Fisher was fretting and in a mood to criticize. As we lunched in our tent he instructed me to wash my hair, which, understandably because of the weather outside, was full of sand. The Intelligence Officer then returned with news about the battle but no gold pencil. Unfortunately the Intelligence Officer had forgotten all about this matter which in his mind was less important than the military situation. The Brigadier's short moustache bristled. Furious he took his Intelligence Officer outside into the sand-storm and sacked him in ringing tones which echoed into our tent. We realized that General Neil Ritchie, commanding the 8th Army, was being slow in making a plan and because of the delay of his attack the Germans were being given time to make gaps in the mine-fields and bring up their supplies. Instead of being used as a fresh Brigade we were split up and distributed piecemeal down to troop formations in other Brigades.

Our Headquarters was left with nothing to command. The Germans were given time to regain the initiative and as they burst out of 'the Cauldron' the British troops encircling them fell back. The Germans moved very fast to Tobruk, where, due to sanded-in minefields and weakened anti-tank defences, the Garrison capitulated. Gerald and I had by this time been transferred to 22nd Armoured Brigade which was commanded by Brigadier Bill Carr. Our orders were to retreat to Matruh and we raced back along the escarpment. But when we reached a point on the escarpment south of Matruh I could see the leading Germans cross the road south of Matruh like horses in a race. I was amazed to see the defences which we had prepared with such care two years before overrun so easily.

Our orders then were to go back to El Alamein. The German units and ours were running neck and neck and at night their leaguers were close to ours. That night as we leaguered in a wadi near Gerawla we were bombed by the RAF and suffered casualties. Next day we managed to reach the security of the defensive boxes at El Alamein prepared by General Auchinleck who had taken over command from General Ritchie. Our Commander-in-Chief came up looking calm and dignified with a very new bedding roll on the back of his staff car. His car stopped and he asked for some directions.

Our position was a strong one composed of a number of boxes straddled in depth across a narrow front. We were protected on our left flank by the Qattara Depression which was impassable to vehicles so that enemy tanks were likely to attack along the escarpment of the Ruweisat Ridge which provided a hard surface. Next day Rommel was able to assemble about thirty tanks and with these he attacked with the sun behind him along the Ridge, hoping to break through before the British had had time to consolidate. The 22nd Armoured Brigade, responsible for defending the Ruweisat Ridge, was luckily reinforced by a squadron of 9th Lancer tanks which arrived at lunchtime. So the attack was repulsed. I heard Brigadier Bill Carr, in whose tank I was sitting, say over the wireless, "We have given them a bloody nose".

At the beginning of July the situation at El Alamein became stable and the German drive towards the Delta was halted. At this time the Greys, now fully mechanized, had arrived from the Delta and were under the command of 22nd Armoured Brigade on their way to the Alamein Box defended by the South Africans. As they were spending the night a kilometre or so down the track from our camp I was able to welcome them. As it happened this was the last time I was able to be with my Regiment. Having spent three happy years with them I felt I was going back to the family and in fact the Colonel, Lugs Twistleton-Wykeham-Fiennes, much loved and respected throughout the Regiment told me there was a place for me in the Regiment as soon as I could return. I was able to see my old squadron, B Squadron, and take a drink off my Squadron Leader, Humphrey Guinness, and his second-in-command, Frank Bowlby, who were sharing a Grant tank. That night the Grant tank was to blow up. Aidan Sprot described what happened in his book *Swifter than Eagles*:

> "An unfortunate thing happened to them here the evening we were going to the Alamein Box to come under the South Africans. Frank was sitting on top of the turret covered in maps, signal forms, attaché cases, earphones, etc, and Trooper 'Duggie' Evans was filling the tank with petrol when 'woomph' and a sheet of flame shot up from the clutch shaft. Frank having disentangled himself from his earphones leapt off and got everyone away. Luckily I was beside the tank when it happened and managed to pull the fire extinguishers but they made no difference. The flames got more of a hold and poor Humphrey and Frank watched their belongings burning inside, including a lovely Canadian fur coat which Colonel Lugs had given Frank at his wedding. Shortly after, we were all sitting around at a conference lit up by the flames eighty yards away, when there was an almighty explosion and the tank blew up, the turret sailing through the air and landing beside us. That was enough, so we moved off straight away as it was a perfect target to any Hun planes."

That night we in Brigade HQ heard a tremendous explosion from the direction of the Greys and the desert shook. Next morning at breakfast time a somewhat crestfallen Humphrey arrived on his way back to Cairo in a jeep. All I could do was to commiserate and offer him a restorative breakfast. This marked the end of Humphrey's time with the Regiment. This was sad. He had a brilliant mind which he had applied to our mechanized training in Honey tanks on the Plains of

Esdraelon around Jenin. Faster tactics had suited him better than the old lumbering horse and inadequate communications. In fact with him on his large charger at the head of the Squadron his troop horses found it difficult to keep up. They were permanently at a jog and became very thin as a result. Humphrey was a charming man, well read and a deep thinker. He was highly strung and had a driving temperament. He had been an international polo player. He always had a look of distraction on his face as if he had just lost his train ticket. Shortly after his lonely departure for Cairo the GOC 1st Armoured Division, General Herbert Lumsden, arrived and when informed of the loss of the Greys tank by his fellow 12th Lancer Brigadier Fisher he was not at all pleased.

The Germans now began consolidating their positions and reorganizing their arms, equipment and supplies. General Auchinleck decided to mount a series of infantry night attacks before the enemy were ready to move on to invade the Nile. We were in a strong defensive position.

On the night of 21 July I was sent as Liaison Officer between 22nd Armoured Brigade and the New Zealand Brigade commanded by Brigadier Clifton. I reported to Brigade Headquarters at about 2000 hours in a Crusader tank equipped with a wireless set by which I hoped to communicate with 22nd Armoured Brigade which was ready to come up in support of the New Zealanders at first light the following morning. Soon after my arrival the New Zealanders went into their attack through the minefields. As soon as the enemy fire became intense I sent my batman, Trooper Edgar of the Greys, who was without armoured protection in my jeep, back to safety. For some miles we followed the Brigadier through the dusk. As it grew dark we moved slowly towards the point of the wedge which had been driven into the enemy line. I then got out of my tank to pee but I got back in again fairly smartly as bullets whizzed past my nose. Next morning at first light we found ourselves trapped in a saucer. Beside us the New Zealand infantrymen were lying in slit trenches which they had dug during the night. German tanks armed with 88 mm guns were firing at us from the ridge in front. The British tanks which should have come to our support at first light were not there. Shells were now landing all round us. I saw a New Zealander dreadfully wounded below the waist crawl pitifully towards my tank. I tried to move the tank to a slightly less exposed position but we were in danger of running the New Zealanders over in their trenches, so I decided to stay still. Our two-pounder gun had no chance against the enemy drawn up in Tiger tanks hull down behind the ridge. Anti-tank gunners of the Northumberland Fusiliers came forward bravely beside us and opened fire. After about half an hour the enemy scored a direct hit on our tank. Smoke and flames came from the engine and my crew of three and I baled out, thankful to be alive and not wounded. I jumped into the nearest slit trench and lay flat on top of a New Zealander who appreciated my protection. After some time the Tiger tanks closed in for the kill. Our Brigade was surrounded and was forced to surrender. Our Brigadier, having taken off his badges of rank, acted as a stretcher bearer and later escaped back to our lines where he reported me as dead. Two of my crew were killed trying to escape on a Bren carrier, which was hit. The other two, myself and one other, without means of escape, were taken prisoner. The German tanks rolled past us, their officers waving us aside as they went past to their next position. We rose from our trenches with arms raised in surrender. We were gradually collected into groups, were formed up and then marched away. We were taken back through the German gun positions which were firing as we passed them. The German soldiers seemed more keyed up in action then our men, their officers barking out their words of command. We were marched back several miles towards El Daba where we were given water and some food and were then forced to lie down in the fierce heat. Some of the New Zealanders were desperately thirsty, having had little to drink since the night operation. Towards evening we were taken on to Daba where we were handed over to the Italians. Several of the German soldiers were envious of our situation. "For you the war is over," they said as they left us to return to the front line.

For me there was a good deal of retrospective anxiety. We had been more or less the only vehicle above ground, with a number of 88s all in close proximity able to take us on as a sitting duck. There was nothing that we could do because I was in a Crusader armed with a little 2-pounder gun which was absolutely useless. It was like a pea shooter at that range. We had a few shots but that didn't do much good, nor would legging it from Lord knows where back to our lines, when probably we would have been picked off anyway. But that wouldn't exactly have gone down too well if the British presence in the form of the Crusader tank had just disappeared at that critical stage. Our presence would have been more useful had we not lost touch with Armoured Brigade Headquarters since the beginning of the attack, due to the jamming of our wireless by the enemy. Had we been more in touch we might have helped our tanks to move up closer behind us in the dark.

I did hear and I have read since that Brigadier Fisher commanding 22nd Armoured Brigade got his map references wrong and did not appear in the right place. So as a result no armour came to save us.

6

In The Bag, Italy

The prisoner of war's first reaction after the battle is probably one of thankfulness to be alive and of having survived. As he leaves the noise of gunfire behind him, he begins to think in terms of peace. Although he is a prisoner and has lost his freedom he feels nevertheless a sense of liberation coming over him. Perhaps the realities of the battlefield have shown him the limitation of his courage. The awareness of the horrors of war are uppermost in his mind. During the battle he has carried out his duties to the best of his abilities with the help of such training as has been given to him during the preceding months. Now fate has stepped in and his life has suddenly and unexpectedly taken a different turn. He can now honourably retire from the battlefield, retire into the privacy of his own being and start to cultivate the hidden resources of the mind. He will meet new people with whom he will share sufferings and during the period of his captivity he will learn a new kind of gregariousness whilst cultivating his own individuality.

For myself I was able to shed the burden of the responsibility of living up to my father's great reputation as a soldier. Now suddenly fate had liberated me. I could slink away into the shadows of a prisoner of war camp to cultivate the resource of painting. This new purpose was to save my morale during my time as a prisoner. Although these thoughts were running vaguely through my mind, they took some time to crystallize. For the time being I had to face the ordeals ahead.

For several days I had been suffering from dysentery and should have reported sick. I felt weak and ill, and as this diarrhoea had lasted a while I was debilitated. I had left my sheepskin coat in the tank and had no other clothing but my shirt and shorts. The night was cold. A kind New Zealander gave me a pullover which kept me warm.

As I lay down to sleep I thought of the gulf that lay between home and myself, and wondered how long the news would take to reach them that I was not dead but a prisoner. I knew that under the rules of the Geneva Convention they would have to be told. There was nothing I could do now but submit, follow the instructions of the Italian guards and accept the new tempo of life. Next day we were driven in diesel trucks along the coast road I had not driven along since my days with General Dick O'Connor. The General had himself been captured sixteen months earlier. We were taken past Ma'aten Bagush to Matruh where we were put in the wire cage constructed by the British in 1940. We had no shade and little food or water. With me were several Tank Corps officers, a member of the Household Cavalry and a number of New Zealanders. We were all tired and miserable.

Then after some time a truck arrived, my name was called and I was told to get in. I was driven back east to Ma'aten Bagush to my old Headquarters to be taken before an Italian officer in an ACV. Behind him were some boxing gloves, an epée and a silk dressing gown. He knew who I was and introduced himself in English as an Italian count who had frequented the world of London society before the war. He asked me some question. I refused to answer except to say my name, rank and number. When I remained silent the officer looked harsh. He said he would give me ten minutes to think things over. When I was brought back and still was silent, he looked grim. He said he admired me but that I must face the consequences. Not knowing what was in store,

I was taken by the guard into one of the dugouts which had been used as an office by the Western Desert Force HQ. The door was then locked. Inside it was cool. An old camouflage net was on the ground. I lay down on it. I was given some excellent risotto in a mess tin. I felt better. Then some time later the door was opened and a dark-skinned officer dressed in RAF uniform came in. I sensed that he was an Italian sent to live beside me as a stooge. His tale sounded plausible. He had made a forced landing ferrying a plane from England. He talked of London and told me who had won the Derby. In fact we got on quite well together. Next day after lunch I was taken into the officers' mess and was given coffee and a liqueur. The Italians tried to break down my reserve, but I managed to keep off all military topics. Whenever my stooge friend tried to discuss the war, I excused myself on the grounds that there might be a dictaphone hidden behind the wall. Apart from information about our forces and equipment in the desert, there was nothing I could have divulged as I had spent the war far from the corridors of power. I knew nothing of the Russian situation, nor of our plans for a Middle East offensive. Next day I felt well enough to bathe, and the stooge and I swam and basked on the same beach where I had swum with the General. Now our troops were far to the east. After about three days, when they had given up all hope of getting any information out of me, I was put in the truck again. When saying goodbye the stooge told me that there had in fact been a dictaphone hidden in the dugout. For a moment I wondered to myself whether I had been indiscreet, but then I felt confident that I had not given any information which could be useful to the enemy.

I was taken back to the cage at Matruh where I rejoined the same batch of officers. Together we began our dreary journey back through Tobruk and Derna to Barce where we spent a few days in huts. I was still suffering from diarrhoea; I was in pain and was weak. The Italian hospital next to us was filled with sick and wounded Italians and short of medicine, so I had no hope of medical attention. I saw the Italian doctor, who could give me nothing. In the bunk below me was a bearded officer called Rene Cutforth, who had been captured serving with the Senussi, and Senussi became his nickname. His lively companionship and his sardonic outlook were to boost my morale during the months ahead. The camp seemed to be full of endlessly washing Indians. I felt too weak to leave my bed. The elation which had come over me after the battle left me. I felt depressed and dejected. This mood got worse after we moved back to a warehouse in Benghazi. There it was dark and claustrophobic. But the troops near us were in worse conditions. They were behind wire in the open sun, many of them dying because of the flies and the dysentery. Our food was revolting – small tins of bully beef which I could not eat, and disgusting ersatz coffee for which we had to queue. A kind officer in the 4th Hussars who was in the bunk below let me save my strength and brought the coffee to me in a tin because I had left my mug in the tank. After three weeks we were flown back to Italy, to a transit camp at Bari, where I teamed up with Cutforth. Here we were given our first Red Cross parcel which was shared between two. Senussi quoted Kropotkin's theory which he said meant "to everyone his share according to his need". Senussi's and my needs were unfortunately not the same. He was hungry and his need was immediate. I felt ill and needed my food little and often. Self-denial over food, as I was to discover gradually, was not Senussi's strong point; his needs were paramount, and the tins of jam and margarine and milk, the biscuits and the potted meat all disappeared with remarkable speed. He had the habit of descending on some unsuspecting POW asking him for a spoonful of sugar in return for two next week then removing his victim's entire week's sugar ration in a huge clawlike spoon specially constructed for tea-stirring. Senussi was an admirable companion and staunch friend, and we were to be partners for over a year. Thanks to Senussi, my morale began to pick up at Bari. I became oblivious to the noise in the barrack huts which went on all day and to the noise of people endlessly tramping past on the way to the lavatory at night. I found some scraps of paper and a pencil and began to draw the sprawling bodies of my fellow prisoners lying almost naked in the sun. I remembered Humphrey Guinness's description of a friend who had been captured in the First World War, who had bounced a tennis ball endlessly against a wall with a stick and who had come home a Wimbledon player. I decided to do the same kind of thing with drawing. This helped to pass the time until, after a period of some weeks, we were taken by train across central Italy to Sulmona in the Abruzzi near Rome.

After leaving the station we marched up the mountain valley towards a camp with red roofs behind high walls and watch towers. This was where Senussi and I were to make our home for the next year. Our new camp was near a village which was called ironically Fonte d'Amore. The new arrivals were put into two large huts in the lower officers' compound. We did not feel over-cramped. We were given battle-dress, overcoats, boots, underclothes, shirts, socks and even pyjamas. We were shown a well-stocked library from which we could take out books. The air was bracing and the light was sparkling in the dry September weather. At that moment for a short time I almost forgot that I was a prisoner and my spirits began to rise.

Prisoners of war roughly divided themselves into five main categories; escapers, creators, administrators, the students and the sleepers. Many individuals combined two or more of these approaches in their system of dealing with captivity. I adopted the second and fourth lines of activity. The escapers plotted in dark corners and dug tunnels, and as a regular soldier I should have joined them.

The administrators' way of life was to provide all the necessary aids to our material wellbeing. They were the housekeepers, the dolers out of Red Cross parcels from the parcel stores. They organized rations and meals, and cooked when there was anything to cook. In Sulmona, where there was scope for initiative because of the black market and the superfluity of lirae in the officers' pockets, the administrators managed to provide not only a reasonable diet but a weekly ration of red wine. The task of dealing with the Italian camp authorities involved much patience and persuasion, since the word '*domani*' was often used and had to be taken at face value. We found later that the Germans were by comparison more co-operative and more reliable in this respect, though they were more conscious of the rules and regulations.

The students were the thirsters after knowledge who attended lectures on almost every subject known to man. Their interests included education, art, science, agriculture, politics and the law. Many of us welcomed the opportunity to learn about matters which had evaded us in peacetime. Some of us were able to develop a talent which might flower after the war. There were quite a few who seemed to do little than lie about, think of the past, and who were unable to find any outlets except perhaps whenever possible to play volleyball or bridge.

The decision as to whether or not to be involved in escaping was taken out of my hands because my continued sickness due to dysentery made me unfit for duty. Because of that I had absolutely no guilty feeling about not doing enough to escape. I could not have escaped because I was not well enough to contemplate living off the land once I was out. If there was to be a chance and I did feel fit enough to take the opportunity to escape I would have done so. Later on at one point on our way back from Italy to Germany I did have an opportunity to escape and I was going to take it and get out that night but fate was against it. For various reasons we got moved on that very day and I didn't get a chance. Just as well as I was still sick.

Soon after my arrival at Sulmona I decided to give a lecture. I chose as my subject "Significant Form" based on a book by Clive Bell. At the conclusion of my talk I overheard one Australian say to another Australian, "I always thought it was a lot of snobbery. Now I know it is." In my researches I had failed to understand the reasons behind this thoughtful book, which focused on geometrical simplicity and overall design in place of the vagueness of impressionist painting. Roger Fry's lectures which I found in the library explained the possibility of enjoying paint for its own sake. The truth of that gradually dawned on me as I began to look in new ways at the mountains beyond the wire, or in the evenings when in spite of the darkness of the hut I peered at figures huddled round the Stufa in the light of our fat lamps. After that I gave no more lectures and my only contribution was as an organizer of art exhibitions. I attended lectures on the merits of alfalfa as opposed to clover given by Colonel Fell, an Australian agricultural scientist, and on the anatomy of the horse by a veterinary surgeon called Jim Phipps. I valued my time for reading and absorbed many books, mostly modern English literature and books on art, which I discussed with Senussi and with the war correspondents Patrick Crosse and Eddie Ward. Entertainment was endlessly provided for me by Senussi, who took a delight in sharing the secrets of his mind. He was a born raconteur and entertainer, who later made a reputation for himself on radio and television under his real name. He loved showing off. Though my role as listener had its drawbacks and could be tiring, I was intrigued by his approach to living. Senussi was not only an artist – he could draw and paint and write – he was also a man of action who had led the Senussi through battles in Abyssinia and the desert in real Lawrence of Arabia style. His experiences in Africa on short rations had left him with a vitamin deficiency which caused his teeth to drop out and gave his face an increasingly emaciated appearance as he lay smoking, dreaming, thinking, reading, talking and drinking endless cups of tea. His own free thinking made him intolerant of the ethics and beliefs which were accepted unquestioningly by the society in which I had been brought up. Senussi's belief in the individuality of man, and in himself, were beliefs for which he had striven in the years before the war, and were for me but theories – theories which would have to be tested in real life outside. Not being politically minded and having grown up in a somewhat sheltered way of life the realities of how other people, particularly the middle classes, had lived their lives had been taken for granted. I had known them but never known what they were really like; if you are living in close proximity with people you begin to understand what makes them tick and what they are like.

Senussi was a most engaging character and I think he did really broaden my whole perspective of life; listening to his well stocked mind was stimulating. If you are cheek by jowl with somebody, whoever it is, you are affected by their personality and mind and I think he did have a lasting effect on me.

Through talking with Senussi I learned of the ways of modern society, of all the various facets well known to us today of shop stewards, trade unions and employers, and I settled down to read and think about new theories of town and country planning. My ideas about politics were widened by the discussions which took place amongst the small circle of Senussi admirers who gathered round his bed. Among them was Hamish St Clair Erskine of the Scots Guards, who believed in the existence of a fundamental understanding between the aristocracy and the working class. In opposition to this view point was Dr Fish, a seedy-looking but amiable medical practitioner from London whose morale seemed to

19. My 21st birthday party, Bemersyde, March 1939. Standing (*left to right*): Jean Ogilvy, Gavin Astor, Ursula Mills, Billy Hartington, Tom Egerton, Debo Mitford, Rodney Berry, Charlie Lansdowne, Billy Ednam, Bridget Elliot, Philip Profumo. Seated: Rene, Xandra, myself with Gyp, Doria, Andrew Scott.

20. Doodle Stanton (see p.68) interrogating Arabs. Colonel Todd is on the left, Lugs Fiennes centre left with walking stick.

21. "I was in a good squadron under George Trotter" (p.67).

22. Sketching near Jenin, 1941.

23. Robin Hastings' shooting party, Safad, 1940 (see p.74). *Left to right*: John Gunn, David Callander, Robin Hastings, Calum Renton, Christopher Sinclair.

24. General Dick O'Connor, General Jumbo Wilson and Brigadier Selby at
    Mersah Matruh, 1940.

25. Peter Halswell (see p.96) at Galilee, 1941.

26. I propose the toast to the Immortal Memory, Haifa, 1941.

27 Self-portrait painted in Colditz.

28. Rene Cutforth painted by me at Hadamar.

29. My painting of Patrick Crosse (*see p. 124*).

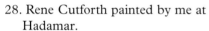

30. Inside the bungalow at Sulmona.

31. "I peered at figures huddled round the Stufa" (*p. 113*).

32. Still Life, 1946.

33. The Cows, 1948.

34. HM The Queen, now the Queen Mother, visits my exhibition in Edinburgh (see p.160).

35. Girl with a Green Hat, 1946.

36. At work at Camberwell, 1946.

37. At the Buccleuch Hunt Ball, 1946.

38. With Paul Maze at Rose Cottage, 1946.

39. At Bemersyde with my daughters Raina and Vivienne, 1961.

depend on the Utopian ideas of the Communist Party. My naivete and my orthodox reactions caused Senussi no irritation and luckily some merriment. I suppose, too, I gave him a sense of power. This could have been harmful to me, but I did not lack self-confidence and had my own resource of painting. I was able to buy some water colours through the Italian black market – in pans, because tubes would have been confiscated due to the possibility of tiny maps being hidden inside them – with which I managed to escape for hours, painting studies of the camp and of my fellow prisoners.

One of our group, a Canadian airman captured at Tobruk called Hugh Heney, had studied the methods of the Impressionists and of Degas. He understood the meaning of weight, of form and movement, and his interpretations of the scene around us were conveyed in terms of light and colour which had more subtlety than mine. By working away from the subject he was able to detach himself and so prevent too literal an approach. Our discussions together were to our mutual advantage and enabled us each in his own way to make progress.

My work was one of the reasons for the turmoil round my bed; paints and drying pages had to compete with socks and odds and ends of washing, and tins of food. This turmoil was a part of the larger turmoil around us, caused by too many men living in a confined space. We lived without silence, though perhaps in the winter evenings when the cold drove us to read in bed by the light of our small fat lamps we had a degree of peace and quiet.

Above us in the top compound lived the privileged minority of Australians, who had the comfort of individual rooms and spring beds. They deserved them, since they had mostly been prisoners longer than we had. The New Zealanders with whom I had been captured had gone to their own camp. Sulmona had originally been established for

Austrian prisoners taken in the First World War and the Australians had priority over us who formed a consignment of British officers among the hordes of prisoners taken in the summer of 1942. We were housed in humbler quarters, below the salt, so to speak. Even further below on the far side of the wall was a vast concourse of huts which contained the other ranks in strict segregation. They were a tighter squeeze than we, and probably a livelier lot. But the Australians were quite lively enough, endlessly energetic with games and sports, and at the same time each fulfilled as individuals with some talent of the mind or hand. They were generous and hospitable and entertained us to parties in their rooms, to games of poker and cups of tea and glasses of wine. Here one evening I met Eddie Ward, a BBC correspondent who had, through an earlier misunderstanding with the Italians, been classified as an other rank and been put in the troops' compound. Some months of greater discomfort among the troops had earned him a place in the more luxurious quarters of the top compound. Eddie was a link with my own background and shared with me an outlook which was separate both from that of the more democratic Australians and from that of my British companions. Eddie shared a room with his fellow correspondent, Anderson, and together they prepared a News Bulletin each day taken from some wireless or newspaper source. Through them we were told of the Battle of Alamein and of the wounding of Richard Wood. Through their contacts with the troops below, they were able to establish the performance of a series of plays and revues by other ranks. These took place in our hall. Seats were reserved and sold for lirae, which helped the other ranks to buy food and props. The officers in their turn put on a pantomine at Christmas, which was a huge success amongst the troops. At Christmas we had a special dinner. The Australians favoured a system of saving up their rations for big meals, and their Christmas dinner was a monumental feast. For weeks, due to the efforts of John Wintour, our buying officer, the ration cart had been seen wending its way up the valley with special black market supplies hidden under the straw. In addition to turkeys and wine, there were bottles of Grappa and also of Ardente described on the label as "Superiore al Whisky". When the big night came, a bar had been installed in one of the huts. Due to a temporary Christmas armistice, the Italian orderly officer was invited to join us. He became so drunk he had to be carried to bed, and two of the guards, unable to go on duty, handed their uniforms and equipment to Bob Ross and another Australian, who finished the job for them. Most of the officers went merrily to bed, not only that night, but every night until Hogmanay.

After Christmas my first private parcel arrived from home, with books and paints chosen by my sisters. They sent me Dunhill tobacco and pipes, and a Greys cap to replace my own left in the tank, and light shoes to replace my heavy army boots. The books were temporarily removed for purposes of censorship and were returned via Rome with their bindings removed.

Once a month during the winter we were taken on walks, though these were in the form of marching through the countryside in fours. Summer brought heat and flies and bed bugs and a good deal of sunshine. Then two little guards came in one day with news of the landings in Sicily. Soon after, towards the end of June, we were told on muster parade by Lieutenant Graziani, an unpleasant officer and nephew of the General, that we were to move north to another camp. Our journey took us along the Adriatic coast. Through the windows of the carriage we saw for the first time for many months the forms of beautiful women sunbathing on the beaches.

After reaching Bologna we were marched to some modern barracks where we were put through a very thorough search. The Carabinieri guards inspected our naked buttocks with the aid of torches in their search for maps. We felt unsettled and restless in our new home. We knew that an armistice with the Italians was imminent. The camp filled up with officers from other camps in the south of Italy. We waited anxiously as the days dragged by. One day a new officer arrived, a dapper Italian cavalryman in boots and breeches with an eyeglass, who had jumped in the Italian equestrian team before the war. One day I happened to hear him addressing a group of British officers with the words "Does anyone here know Lord Hardweeck?". As I happened to know Lord Hardwicke I volunteered my name. He immediately saluted and introduced himself as Count Palastrelli. For several days afterwards I was supplied with eggs, until suddenly we heard the news of the Italian armistice which had been signed on 8 September 1943. When the news came there was wild excitement throughout the camp both among the Italians and ourselves.

Brigadier Mountain, our senior British officer, told us that although we were free to leave camp and the guards had gone, he advised us to remain. A War Office order had been received instructing officers to remain in their camps for the time being. He had been promised a warning from the Italians in case of any German move to take us over. So with this advice we went to bed fully clothed and with our bags packed ready for an immediate move. In the early hours of the following morning we were woken by the sound of machine guns. The Germans had surrounded the camp. We were caught. Desperately we tried to escape, but the Germans had planned their operation so well that we were all rounded up. Two of our officers were found wounded, one of them so severely that he later died. Apart from that, the operation had been blood-less. We were prisoners once more. Our disappointment was terrible. We felt badly let down. The prospect of moving to Germany was grim. Our only consolation was the fact that we were not alone. In front of us between the two wires stood our former Italian guards. One of them, Count Palastrelli, said to one of our officers, "Now we are both in the sack together". I doubt whether he got a civil reply.

At Bologna the SS herded us into cattle trucks, over forty officers in each truck. We were filled with bitter disappointment. We were being moved in depressing circumstances because we had expected freedom after the Italian surrender in September 1943, only to have our expectations transformed into German captivity. We had been always thankful, when we were in Italian camps, that we had the sun. We had lots of advantages and we knew that life in Germany was going to be pretty depressing. We were going into a grey climate with not too much light at the end of the tunnel. And indeed there were a lot of difficulties ahead.

As we waited our turn to be loaded, Senussi managed to get some hot water from the engine driver, hot enough to make tea. With over forty officers in each truck there was little room to spread out. The only light was from a small window in one corner at head height. When the train started we tried to cut a hole through the floor, but found a metal plate lining the wood, so for us escape was impossible. As our journey took us on towards the north, towards the Brenner Pass, we met the mountains at Verona. As the train began to climb towards Trento it went more slowly. One of our officers climbed on to the shoulder of another and dived head first through the window, wide enough for his shoulders to pass. After he dived we heard no more. Some time later the train stopped and the guards ordered us out: "*Raus, Raus*" in angry tones. The train had stopped at a small station. As we piled on to the platform we were hurriedly counted. The SS looked grim and tense. A guard told me that many officers had escaped from those trucks which had wooden floors. We heard after that more than a hundred officers had escaped during the journey between Verona and Trento. In one truck an officer had managed to squeeze through a hole in the floor, crawl along the rods underneath until he reached the side of the train, where he climbed up and slid back the latch of the unlocked truck. As the train climbed slowly up the mountainside most of the officers were able to jump out in turn. In other trucks some officers had boldly crawled through the holes they had made and simply fell or jumped on to the line. For them, unless the train had been going slowly enough to crawl free, there was an almost certainty of being crushed, as the last vehicle, an electric engine, had very little clearance. A few other officers had dived through the window. A large number had survived. Some escaped over the mountains to Switzerland; some were recaptured. The officer in charge of the SS guard now threatened to shoot those officers who had been found in trucks from which there had been a mass escape. They were prevented from doing so by a threat made by our interpreter that for every British officer shot ten SS men in Britain would be shot as a reprisal. In the face of this warning the officer did nothing, though he re-alized he would be punished at the end of the journey. We were now put back in the train. Officers who were in damaged trucks were put into the other trucks, where the crush was even worse. For those of us who had dysentery the conditions became grim. The train journey took us through Bolzano and over the Brenner Pass down to Innsbruck and the Salzkammergut on the other side. Girls in dirndls waved as the train went by. Soldiers manning an ackack gun on a truck behind us had found a gramophone on which they played Viennese waltzes. As my gaze fastened on this landscape which I had known and loved before the war, listening to the nostalgic strains of the Blue Danube, my heart sank at the thought of what was to come.

The train jerked its way slowly round Munich until it reached Moosburg, some thirty miles north-east on the flat land beyond. We got out stiffly on to the platform beside the fir trees. Being one of the last to get out, I volunteered to help unload the supply of Red Cross parcels which we had brought with us. As the others were marched off by the guards, I was left relatively on my own and I managed to get into conversation with the engine driver who volunteered his anti-Nazi views and his hopes for an allied victory. This came as a revelation to me. Due to reading the papers full of propaganda, I had no idea until then of the amount of opposition to the Führer. I quickly seized a Red Cross parcel and gave it to the driver, scribbled a note and asked him to take it to my old friends in Munich. This he promised to do and, thinking no more about it, I went on piling the parcels on to some handcarts which we then trundled through the wood towards the camp. In an earlier chapter I have described the successful result of my message to Munich, more successful than I had anticipated in that it enabled me to meet one of the German guards whom I had known before the war who was able to contact the Stengel family who as a result married the elder daughter. In this transaction I had taken on the rôle of Cupid in the land of the enemy.

Moosburg was a huge camp full of French working Commandos and of Russians. The Russians were starving and, with no Red Cross organization behind them, were suffering badly. The SS had handed us over to the Wehrmacht, who were running the camp, and a German officer welcomed us with the usual stiff formalities. Having been searched, we were taken to some wooden huts which we were to share with the French. The French did their best to make us welcome. They had created an atmosphere which, in spite of the surroundings, had a French style. On one of the walls there was a mural painting. There were delicious smells coming from a cooking pot and we soon began to talk about painting.

After a few days one of the Frenchmen, a *chef de barraque*, offered me a chance to escape. He promised to get in touch with some underground organization working in the Munich area and to warn them to look after me. He would supply me with a French tunic in which I could travel relatively easily through Bavaria, where Frenchmen were free to live and work on the land. It would be fairly easy for me to get out of the camp. I would then have to try and jump on to a goods train and hide myself in a truck during the journey to Munich. Once I got to Munich my knowledge of the city would help me to find the main station where I would be hidden away in a sealed Red Cross truck which would be returning empty to Switzerland. We would be handled by French prisoners who were going about relatively guard-free, and who were running the return of these empty trucks. As I was allowed to take someone with me, I approached Patrick Crosse with whom I had begun to establish a friendship, to tell him of the plan. He agreed to come with me and we went to the Frenchman who gave us our French tunics and told us to prepare to escape on the evening of the next day. Our excitement became intense. Although we had eaten little we had no appetite to eat our meagre ration. Our minds, inured to the slow tempo of prison life, now became suddenly alive. Our hearts beat furiously and we felt sick with anticipation. But at the next morning roll call the German officer announced that we were to leave that day. This prevented our chance of escape. Another officer, George Millar, took our place a week or so later and did get through with great difficulty. He got home after an adventurous trip which he described in a book called *Horned Pigeon*. Meanwhile in pouring rain my friends and I waited in columns to be loaded into cattle trucks. The journey took us to Strasbourg where our party divided and some of us were taken to a transit camp at Offenburg. From there we were moved on again northwards. Our train passed through Mannheim during an air raid and came to a halt. As we lay listening to the bombs I suddenly heard an English voice calling from the track below asking who we were. Before he had had time to establish his identity the train moved on and we never discovered who he was nor where he came from.

Next day we reached Hadamar, east of Koblenz, where, because it was too late to unload, we had to spend another night in the cattle trucks.

Next morning we climbed up to an ugly neo-gothic schloss which stood on the hill above the station.

7

Oflag XII B, Hadamar

During our time at Sulmona Senussi and I had been close friends. We had shared parcels and shared companionship. Senussi looked like a prophet; he was versed in literature from Plato to Blake and he had explored Beethoven, Buddhism and witchcraft. He was an exponent in beer-making and would have been good at drinking it as well had any of it been to hand. He introduced me to the lectures of Roger Fry and passed a lot of time drawing but limited himself to the theme of the mask which he executed in a thin cubistic line. As he did this the expression of his toothless suffering face became less wracked. For much of the time when he was not sitting cross-legged drinking tea and reading a book Senussi enjoyed describing people he had encountered in his not uneventful life to as many people as were willing to listen. The captive audience who used to listen to Rene Cutforth on TV will understand the reason for our readiness to listen to his stories in those days. He was a wonderful companion, which was as well as he hated to be alone, and did at times fall into states of deep depression. By now our relations had begun to fray and one morning our shared shaving water tin flew, so Eddie Ward took my place beside Senussi who needed a stronger, more aware and more articulate partner to stand up to him. I joined forces with Patrick Crosse who, like me, remained slightly aloof from the herd.

After our arrival at Hadamar I felt depressed for some time

in the dreary atmosphere of our gothic castle. As always when I moved to another camp I found myself adrift. There were no books and I found myself stuck there with nothing very much happening. My whole routine had gone. Depression and boredom really set in.

For a time after our move we had no books, no parcels and no paints. The damp, cold German autumn with its lowering skies did not help our spirits to rise and Patrick and I walked round the compound below the castle together exchanging the secrets of our private worlds. Our friendship enabled us to put our hardship into perspective and gave us a necessary detachment from our fellow prisoners.

With Eddie Ward and Jim Phipps we shared a room with some South Africans. After a while Patrick and Eddie and I moved upstairs to a large room at the top of the schloss, where we joined Senussi and four others and settled down to an ordered existence. Our comforts were restored, first through some parcels lent by the prisoners at Spangenburg and then by a new supply of our own Red Cross parcels. Of all the camps I was in during my time as a prisoner Hadamar was the dreariest. It was largely composed of older British and South African officers. For some reason a number of younger officers, myself included, had been sent to Hadamar. The officers as a whole were middle-aged, and there was not an enormously lively atmosphere in the place. One of the officers, sadly, was to die during the coming winter. Another of our number had been already locked up as a POW during the First World War. Eddie Ward spent hours each day listening to the German news from which he prepared reports to be read out each evening behind closed doors. In this work he was helped by a Czech doctor who stood with his ear glued to the loud-speaker in the dining room while dictating the resumés in gutteral English to Eddie below. Poor Doctor Gottlieb hated the Germans with a consuming loathing and was in the habit of committing his thoughts to a private diary. One day during a search the diary was discovered and Doctor Gottlieb was sentenced to a ten-day stint of solitary confinement for, as the notice from the Commandant on the camp notice board told us, "describing my parades as a military nonsense and bullshit".

In order to enable artists to explore the landscape outside I was responsible for securing permission for a series of weekly sketching walks on parole. To start with the sketchers were genuine and in small numbers. Gradually non-sketchers got to hear, and it was incredible how popular these walks became. Our ranks swelled as we set out each week and swelled even more as we returned with pockets and artists' holdalls bulging with apples and other provender gathered from the trees and fields around. One day, as I was busy with my work oblivious of everything other than the subject before me, I was approached by the guard. I looked up and realized that I was alone. My fellow sketchers had vanished from the scene. In vain I tried to explain that subjects were hard to find and might be anywhere. My explanations were useless and the walks were stopped. After the cessation of our sketching walks I had to concentrate on portraiture. Many officers sat for me and I was able to paint them in oils which had been supplied by the Red Cross. Some musical instruments were also sent and one of the South African officers was able to form a small orchestra which gave regular concerts in the hall.

We listened to gramophone records, Grieg's Piano Concerto and Beethoven's Archduke Trio, which had been bought by Senussi and Eddie.

We also listened to the sound of bombers flying over us on their way to Frankfurt, Giessen and Schweinfurt. From our talks with the guards it was clear that German morale was dropping and that almost all of them longed for us to bring the war to an end. Below in the station the trains were fitted up with large slogans saying *"Sieg oder Bolschevismus"*, a stern reminder to the German people of the alternative to victory.

Once a month a special train came in, delivering a load of old and disabled people who were helped out of the train by nurses, who led them limping to the hospital on the hill beyond. Each morning a number of coffins were taken to a grave among the trees at the top of the hill. We saw no train leave the station carrying departing patients. This seemed suspicious, inexplicable and menacing, but we did not realize at the time that this was part of an appalling tragedy visited upon people who were marked out as being worthless in the Third Reich. After the war Hadamar Hospital was one of the black spots in the list of atrocities which came before the War Crimes Tribunal.

As winter grew cold we were given central heating and we in the top room found ourselves the recipients of not only the warmest air but a plague of fleas which tormented us at nights. Our room became a power house of creativity. Eddie and several others put on a series of plays. Patrick prepared a weekly current affairs programme with elaborate maps pinned up to describe the Russian advances. Senussi edited a magazine called LAG to which he contributed the leading articles and a series of caricatures. One of them depicted me in a feature in the birth column announcing "the arrival of Haig's Round Worm".

Those with enough energy played volley ball in the playground below the schloss. The games were precarious in that when the ball went out of court it was apt to roll towards the wire. Once it had reached the inner wire it was beyond recall and anyone trying to collect it did so at his peril. One day an unfortunate South African did this at a time when the guard who happened to be on duty in the tower was an ardent and hysterical Nazi. Several shots were fired and the South African fell wounded to the ground. This attempt at cold-blooded murder in the middle of the afternoon came as a great shock to everyone present. Otherwise the Germans supervised our routine lives with punctiliousness. Twice a day at Appel they inspected and counted us on the parade ground. For the average prisoner these were our only contacts with the Germans, and for the rest of the day we were left free to lead our lives as best we could. Those of us who had been captured in the desert had their own approach to being a prisoner. We wanted to preserve our individuality and not look like everyone else. Under our senior British officer, Brigadier Mountain, we were given reasonable freedom of dress. We could wear scarfs and many of us wore cap comforters rather than caps on roll call. After the arrival of senior officers who had been captured at St Valery led by General Victor Fortune, Commander of the Highland Division, we were told to dress properly on parade. We had to wear polished boots and army caps in order to impress the Germans and to improve our morale. Our easy democratic way of running the camp was altered, the easy relationship which had existed between the Germans and ourselves was upset. A rift appeared between the Camp Commandant and the new senior British officer. About this time I was sent for by the General, who told me that I was not smart enough on parade and that other senior officers particularly the Australians thought that the son of the Field Marshal should be showing a better example. These events happened during the lengthening days of spring. The allied bombers were flying in increasing numbers overhead. Soon the long-awaited landings in Normandy took place and the announcement of the plot to assassinate the Führer showed us that the end was not far off. Our spirits rose.

At the beginning of November I was again sent for by General Fortune who told me: "The Germans say because you are your father's son you are going to be taken to a more comfortable place". With little warning I had to pack and to be ready that same evening. An order had come through from the High Command of the Wehrmacht instructing the Commandant to dispatch me with two guards to a camp near Leipzig. Patrick Crosse was allowed to come with me to the station and sadly I said goodbye. The journey east took us through Frankfurt and Leipzig and in both places we had to enter air raid shelters because of air attacks. The German civilians looked apathetic and ill but were in no way hostile to me dressed in my khaki uniform.

On my arrival at Colditz I was put into a cell with two beds. Next morning when I awoke I saw George Lascelles in the bunk below. He had arrived during the night. After thorough searches, we were taken through a door into a courtyard milling with prisoners. It was 11 November, exactly twenty six years since the signing of the Armistice.

8

Colditz, The Privileged Nightmare

Whereas at Hadamar we had been housed in a mock gothic schloss, here at Colditz we were in a genuine mediaeval fortress built upon the rock. Instead of being part of a relatively elderly community whose members were living virtually in cold storage, here was a group of much younger men, all living vitally in one way or another. The castle was like a beehive full of cells humming with bees of many kinds.

The bees had all been selected by the Germans for special guarding because of their escape records. The majority were British army officers, but amongst them were sailors and merchant navy men as well as Poles, Dutch, Belgians, French and Americans. As we arrived through the main door from the guard room many of them were walking round the compound. They were hungry-looking but animated and with an eager spirit. Lack of food had not deprived them of energy of thought. Though many of them were distinguished soldiers, the variety of their dress showed they did not suffer from regimentation. All of them were dedicated escapers, but their days of tunnelling were over. The Germans were now in a desperate situation and they had warned that there would be serious danger for any prisoners caught escaping. As the war was reaching its final stages and as the prisoners were so under-nourished that they had little energy the escaping programme had been called off. Their spades and their boxes of piled up rubble had been put away, but although there was an end to their escaping activity, there was no vacuum. Because many of them were distinguished in other spheres and there were members of a variety of professions, so POW's occupied themselves with reading, painting, the theatre and listening to records. There was in this stimulating community a wonderful spirit which had nothing of the rigid régime which had been established at Hadamar. Numbers of them kept emerging from the doorways at the foot of the spiral stairways which connected with the dormitories, and I was taken to one of these dormitories to meet John Elphinstone, who told me as much as he knew about the Prominente.

A number of prisoners with distinguished connections had been brought to Colditz for special guarding. We were segregated at night and were not allowed into the outer compound for recreation. We supposed that Hitler had some purpose behind this arrangement, but in the meanwhile we could do nothing but await developments. Douglas Bader came in towards the end of our conversation, alert and on the lookout for any information that he could find about what was happening in the world elsewhere.

With a driving personality Douglas found it hard, even with his artificial legs, to sit still. His whole being was hungry for action. We were then joined by Miles Reid, a veteran from the First War, who had been captured with the Reconnaissance Regiment – the Phantoms – near the Corinth Canal in 1941 and had been two years at Colditz. He had been sent by the senior British officer, Colonel Willy Tod, to see me to explain that as it was the 11th of November a lecture on my father was to be given that evening. The lecture, given by Stephen Wright of the 9th Lancers, was to be based on Duff Cooper's life of my father which was in the library. Screwy Wright was no great expert on military history, and in order to avoid being upset I was advised not to attend.

I then went off to meet a number of old friends, among whom I found Charlie Forester whom I had not seen since Stowe days. He was suffering from the loss of his spectacles, which was a serious handicap to someone as blind as he was; so he had little to do but walk round the compound, since reading was not possible.

I was invited to become a member of a small mess whose membership included Michael Riviere, a friend from Oxford. Our mess pooled parcels which were used to supplement the meagre German diet. At night the Prominente were locked up in three rooms. Charlie Hopetoun, who had been sleeping in the small single room, offered it to me. Hankering after the privacy it would give me in a life where there was too much company, I accepted his offer. I needed respite from the noise which was the consequence of close daily living. Charlie Hopetoun moved into the larger room next door with John Elphinstone, nephew of the Queen, and George Lascelles, nephew of the King, whilst Giles Romilly and Michael Alexander shared the third room. Giles was the nephew of Mrs Churchill and Michael had pretended to be Field Marshal Alexander's nephew in order to save himself from being shot. Our party had a curious appearance when seen as a whole, and had little of the glamour that one might expect from people with such distinguished connections. Giles looked the part of the romantic poet in spite of his dumpy frame muffled in sweaters. He felt deeply, he had a great understanding of humanity, and a witty sense of humour. He loved drinking endless cups of tea while ruminating to himself. Charlie was more debonair and gay. In addition to his activities in the theatre, he had recently become interested in philosophy. John Elphinstone looked like a soldier and was militarily the senior one among us and gave us a lead upon which we could rely at difficult times. George was too much a hedonist not to mind our privations, and was too new a prisoner to have learnt to curb feelings which he did his best to hide as he settled down to Grove's Musical Dictionary and to his gramophone. Max de Hamel, whom the Germans considered to have some common ancestry with Mr Churchill, was extremely selfless, as was suitable for the calling of the church for which he was preparing. Michael was too much a man of action to take kindly to prison. Behind his urbanity he hid an awareness of the potential dangers of our position, which I personally preferred to keep buried at the back of my mind.

These were my new friends, forced on me by fate, who would none the less become true friends. One of them, Giles Romilly, was destined to become my best man, and I his. Three of them, Charlie, John and Giles, had endured periods of imprisonment which were beginning to do damage. During my first few days I felt unsettled, as if on my first term at a new school. I felt isolated in my new room. I was in a small cell with a table, chair and bed. Outside the barred window was edged with white paint for ease of identification and, if necessary, marksmanship. I began to long for the company, even the coughing and talking, of my friends at Hadamar. The guards marched stamping up and down the passage outside, stopping at intervals to peer through the spyhole in my door. Through the small barred window of the cell I could see a sheer drop down the rock face with a series of barbed wire fences which lay between the castle and the woods beyond. The wire fences were covered by a number of watch towers and wooden walkways which were patrolled by the guards. The whole scene was illuminated by searchlight and gave an eerie feeling. During the day we spent our lives around the courtyard, where guards were scarce, although quite large numbers of guards did emerge at times of appel or to carry out a search.

I was to spend three months in that cell locked up ten hours a night during a winter of extreme physical privation. The temperature fell to minus 15 degrees centigrade, and though there was a stove in the cell, the German ration of coal was too meagre to let me use it. During that time the supply of Red Cross parcels ceased. On my arrival our mess had to rely on its shrinking supply of reserve tins, but by Christmas these too had gone. The German rations were likewise cut down, so that we were living on a starvation diet, so low that the Germans themselves were anxious and weighed us all. These privations coupled with an intense spiritual awareness which came partly from my work and partly from anxiety about our future – and because I was sleeping monklike and alone – induced in me a heightened mental state akin to mysticism, so that as I lay awake my mind focused upwards along strange beams of light. I happened to be reading Aldous Huxley, whose thoughts about mysticism made me more aware of my experiences. Having experienced these visions, I can see the reason for the hair shirts which are necessary adjuncts to saint-hood. The morale of the prisoners, as they trod round the cobbled courtyard in Van Gough fashion, was high. Though there was a setback due to the German attack in the Ardennes, we all knew that the end of the war could not be very far off. Most of us managed to find some interest which enabled us each day as we awoke to have something on which to focus our attention. During my time at Colditz I continued to paint a number of portraits of Jock McCulloch, of Michael Alexander and of Michael Riviere. I also painted a portrait of myself, which I had to paint sitting in the lavatory which contained our only mirror, working with some interruptions because of the needs of my companions. I also painted a large snow landscape of the scene from the window of our mess. I was helped at the time by reading a book by André L'Hôte called *Le Traité du Paysage*, and by discussions with David Stirling, the leader of the SAS, who had studied as a pupil of L'Hôte in Paris before the war. There was no shortage of paints, and to the irritation of my less artistic companions, parcels of oils and brushes and canvas boards sent by the Red Cross continued to arrive at a time when our supply of food and tobacco dried up. Their fury did not seem to abate when on one occasion these parcels were accompanied by a collapsible chapel.

My regular work, which involved a practical use of my hands, was an ideal therapy, a therapy which after the war I was to advocate for the inmates of our civilian gaols. Through the exercise of my craft and through the study of people and of places around me, I was prevented from too much introversion. In spite of this, according to Giles Romilly, I was showing some strange symptoms as I left my cell to join him and Michael in their room. He wrote of me:

> "At ease with his long thin feet on the warm porcelain blue tiles of the cupboard-high German stove, a book upon his lap, he would go into a brown study. He was not in any ordinary sense looking for company; it was rather as if the neighbourhood of people provided a comfort like the heat of the stove. He had no casually fluent or anecdotal chat. His isolated sentences were usually pictures, dark and deep in tone, of some facet of his experience."

According to Giles I had been affected by my experiences as a prisoner:

> "Well before the time of his arrival in Colditz Dawyck had stabilized his prisoner depression. It was trained like an obedient dog and was under his control. Nevertheless, captivity had affected him more severely than was common, certainly more severely than it had affected the other Prominente. There were reasons. One was the superficial frailty of a constitution helpless against recurrent dysentery, and gastric miseries aggravated by prisoner food which it could never accommodate. Then too Dawyck was a child of the Border country, his home looked out over the Tweed and its wild country and he had grown up out of doors, striding with long legs over the hills and far away in any weather. The

sports of the country had been his pleasures: and his time at Oxford, with the OTC, a history degree achieved not too arduously, and clubs and more sport, had seemed only a pleasant extension of that Border background, and a palatable prelude to the soldier's life by which Dawyck intended, with no apparent shadow of doubt in himself, and certainly none in his family, to follow his famous father's example. For three years, even in the Middle East, things had continued in this light. Most of that time his Regiment was still horsed. Then came the sudden moment in which everything changed. The effort of adjustment, the acclimatization to shackled movement, starved eye, and uncooperative constitution, had exposed in Dawyck's temperament a sombre side whose surface might otherwise have remained hidden. But this had brought with it, as if in redress, depth of perception that was sometimes startling, and always interesting."

In order to give some antidote to my caged feeling, I was one of the Prominente who took advantage of the parole walks which were offered to us to compensate us for not being allowed out into the recreation area. On these walks we were escorted by a Feldwebel and four guards armed with tommy guns. When asked the reasons for the arms, the Germans replied that they were to protect us from the civilian population. More likely they were intended as a deterrent against any rescue operation which might be mounted from home. In spite of the guards and of the fact that I had to dress up for them because John Elphinstone took the view that we should not let the Germans think they were getting us down, these walks were a real refreshment for me.

Towards the end of January we received a supply of Red Cross parcels which were sent to us as a result of pressure from Miles Reid, who, repatriated for health reasons, was able to warn the Red Cross of our serious plight. We then had enough parcels to justify a distribution of a full half-parcel to each officer. This windfall coincided with some new arrivals which added more difficulties to our housekeeping. First came General Bor Komorowski and five Polish generals who had led the abortive rising in Warsaw during the previous autumn. This arrival necessitated the compression of the Prominente into one room. My solitary confinement came to an end. The other arrival was that of a thousand French officers who had walked some eighty-five miles from camps in the east, bringing with them few possessions and little nourishment. All they had to offer was the quality of their minds, and they had a stimulating effect on our social and intellectual lives. This was some compensation for their terrible smell which, due to the shortage of our hot water, they were unable to remove. Unwashed and with little food, they bedded down on straw in passages around the yard. Because I was a painter, and perhaps also because of the esteem in which my father's name was held in France, I soon became somewhat of a centre of attraction and received a number of social calls which, because my French guests had little to occupy their time, took some time and digressed into many channels of conversation. A typical conversation during one of these Colditz social visits was described by Giles Romilly when I was talking to Captain Binet. In reply to my remark, *"Il n'y a pas de couleur maintenant . . .* Often when there is no colour one is depressed and when one is depressed one paints the most gay and happy things possible."

Binet replied rather inconsequentially, "Oh yes, the camps are often just as interesting to paint in winter as in summer."

Among the French who had arrived was Jean Guitton, a philosopher and a Christian dedicated to finding bridges between believers and non believers. He had been a close friend of the 2nd Lord Halifax, an Ecclesiastical Commissioner for England and a high churchman. Trained as a journalist, he was to become a leading writer on religion and philosophy. He would become a close friend of Pope Paul VI and a confidant in France of Mitterand and Pompidou. He would be elected to the Acadamie Française. He would be an advocate of Christian Unity and would try to heal the rift between the Catholic church and the French Catholic fundamentalists led by Monsieur Lefebvre.

"My first contact was with the son of Field Marshal Haig, a tall young man, pale and frail, with the eyes of a wild deer. He had a moustache like those of our father's at the beginning of the century, with the ends slightly curled upwards, which gave him a fine air. He had a gentleness which was incredible in a captain who was the descendant of a long line of captains of war. I was sure without having any proof that the Field Marshal had married a woman who was a tender woman full of pathos, who had loved him passionately because she was his opposite, and that the son was the portrait of and the continuation of his mother. He talked little about strategy except to say in a voice which was deep and true that the German army was broken. But he was a great lover of painting, and in his corner near a barred window through which an occasional ray of light appeared, he had installed a studio. He found consolation in his paints."

Jean Guitton also painted, mostly scenes from the Bible, and he was later to paint landscapes in the Holy Land. His interpretations were generalized and expressionistic – painting in the French manner and the result of deep inner feeling. In the words of the Master Paul Cézanne, *"La peinture c'est une méditation le pinceau à la main"*.

He referred to me and to Colditz in his book *La Derrière Heure*. A conversation on the subject of paintings of The Crucifixion led to my suggesting how the head and the hands could be drawn. Jean Guitton was never to pay heed to anatomy or visual accuracy so any advice I offered was probably taken for information only and used as a literary device to heighten the description of our meetings:

"In listening to Lord Haig I thought about his work, and the fact that however perfect it might be, it would be obscured by the ideas one had about his birth – that the laurels of the father would weigh heavily on the freedom of the son. If you are provided with a glorious heritage at your birth you are less capable of providing yourself with a way of life which is your own. And I said to myself, how could he succeed in a vocation which is so contrary to that of his father – a vocation which has to do not with battles but with thinking and more subtle than thinking – with nuances? To me Lord Haig had a frightening simplicity and a shyness which was full of mystery."

At the close of the winter the news became really good. The Russians were advancing on the Eastern Front, and the Americans were advancing towards us from the West. The tension in the camp became very great, a tension which was heightened for the Prominente because of the precariousness of our situation. Our position was particularly perilous and I didn't dwell on that very much. Every now and again I would have a sort of visual picture of a nasty noose, and then I would put it out of my mind but we did know that we weren't there for nothing and our continued residence on this planet was not necessarily guaranteed.

I shared the anxieties mainly I think with Michael Alexander who dwelt on the subject more often and reminded one of this thought rather more often than I wanted. I think it very much affected Charlie Hopetoun. He was very worried about it and I think it probably worried him to the extent that he became quite ill and he had a breakdown just at the end.

We were determined to find out why the Germans were keeping the Prominente under special guard and when in early February a senior diplomat from Berlin came down to persuade General Bor to order his Polish home forces to capitulate – a hopeless mission because the General was adamant – I decided to take the opportunity to meet our visitor, Baron von Beninghausen. During our talk, though I realized that the Baron was not a staunch Nazi, I saw that he was unreliable and that his assurances meant nothing. He promised to do all in his power to see that the Prominente were not moved. The only promise which he did fulfil was to arrange for the delivery of a parcel of gramophone records for George Lascelles. Because of my anxiety and remembering my experiences at Bologna, I decided to ask to see the Commandant. The Commandant, whose name was Prawitt, was equally evasive; he told me that he had been trying to get the OKW to promise not to hand us over to the SS, but he was not hopeful about the chances of getting such an undertaking.

We did not have to wait much longer in a state of suspense. On 12 April we heard the sound of distant American gunfire. On the same day the Commandant warned us that the Prominente were to be moved that night. Our fears now became very great. We now knew that we were going back to join the last remnants of the Nazi forces. We knew that Hitler was likely to use us as hostages. What had simmered for months in the backs of our minds had now become a reality, a reality which was hard to face.

9

Königstein

On the orders of Hitler and Himmler we were taken away from Colditz. We had little alternative but to comply with the German order. The senior British officer, Colonel Tod, had done his best to help us by threatening the Commandant with dire punishment after the war if he handed us over in violation of the Geneva Convention, which stipulated that we be given twenty-four hours notice and be told our destination. The Commandant had merely replied that as the SS were in the neighbourhood he would be coerced into carrying out his order if he tried to evade it. It is said that Willie Tod should have done more to protect us and have refused to let us go, but there was nothing he felt he could do. He was an immensely nice man. He never received an award or decoration for having been senior British officer through all those very difficult times. He richly deserved one.

Tod had offered to let us lie up, hoping that we would not be found before the Americans' arrival. We had decided not to hide since it would have brought reprisals on the heads of the other prisoners, reprisals which might well have been in the form of shooting because the Germans were desperate.

It seemed to be an inevitable part of the play and it really was a very Wagnerian scene. It was nighttime and we were led out not knowing where to. Everybody was craning out of windows and cheering.

Just before midnight another Prominente, John Winant, son of the American Ambassador in London, was added to our group. Then General Bor Komorowski and the other Poles, John Winant and the rest of the Prominente were all taken outside where we had to listen to an official order being read out by one of the German officers. After that we walked slowly across the dimly lit courtyard from whose windows craned the heads of our fellow prisoners. With the sound of their cheers of encouragement and support in our ears, we passed through the prison gates to find a double line of SS soldiers with tommy guns who formed a passage leading to two buses in which we were driven off with two outriders on motorbikes in front and an armoured car behind. The clock struck midnight as we drove through the town. It was now Friday, 13 April.

We were ignorant of the strategic designs of the super-power in whose name some minion at OKW was moving our bus from Colditz southwards, just as he was probably ignorant of the speed with which the Third Reich was about to collapse. Perhaps I should not use the word 'minion' since telegrams and orders from OKW were said to be signed by Himmler in the name of Adolf Hitler himself, who had some special intention for us. Even though knowing the game was lost, he was determined to move us like pawns across the map of Germany. Hitler was in Berlin. The head of the dragon was about to be cut off by the two armies advancing from east and west. The swift closing of the pincers at a point on the Elbe to the north of us was to precipitate Hitler's death and to save us.

We in a later epoch have pictures in our minds of what happened to the Jewish hostages at the Olympic Games in Munich. We saw photographs of them being driven off by bus and they, just as we did, looked apathetic and in a mood of numb desolation. We had no knowledge of the wider spectrum as we were driven off through the night. We did not know of the jaws of the trap which were about to snap together separating Berlin from the armies in the south. We did not realize that Hitler was about to die after handing over the reins of government to Admiral Doenitz. Even so it was a near thing. Hitler is said to have ordered our execution during his last days in the Bunker.

Our bus took us through Dresden, at least through what remained of Dresden after the raid. We drove through endless wastes of empty ruins looking eerie in the moonlight, and after some time stopped on the outskirts near a public park. Here a lit-up tram full of workers went past us towards the city, the only sign of humanity we had so far seen. Our journey continued for about thirty miles until we began to climb upwards. Then, when the bus could go no further, we got out, and as we did so we saw towering above us a fortress like Edinburgh Castle but on a higher rock. Then we began to climb on foot, helping Charlie, who was in no fit state and who had been roused from his drugged sleep the night before. Our tortuous climb took us along a path, through an outer gate of the castle wall, through a tunnel, up a wooden ramp to a great archway. Here we paused, and then, entering a small door at the side, found ourselves climbing steps which led us finally to the top of the rock. We came out onto a great wide terrace, from which a vast panorama was visible in the early morning light. We were in the fortress of Königstein.

With these wide perspectives opened to us, the claustrophobia of our recent experiences disappeared. We entered a new world of German Fantasy. The reality of the night before became obliterated by a new unreality. We were welcomed by a group of Wehrmacht officers who, with great courtesy and much saluting, showed us our rooms. Here for a while we rested. Later we were taken to a large low drawing room, panelled and hung with chamois heads and other sporting trophies, and with a portrait of the Führer at one end, where the Germans offered us coffee and rolls and did their best to thaw the atmosphere. One of them, Baron von Friesen, talked about the Stengels with whom I had stayed in Munich before the war. Then the Commandant, Colonel Hesselmann, came in and announced in solemn tones the news that had just been received over the wireless of the death of President Roosevelt. Suddenly we all stood up, Germans and British together, in a moment of sad silence. Afterwards Colonel Hesselmann took us out on to the ramparts and with pride and genuine kindness pointed out the view across the great valley of the Elbe below. He showed us at the end of his garden an 18th century cannon which faced out towards the east whence the Russians were destined to appear in some days' time.

Then for the rest of the day we were left alone in our strange vacuum, uncertain of what would happen. Next morning John Elphinstone was told that orders had come through from OKW for our immediate transfer south. John, knowing what would happen, had the day before decided to press the Germans to keep Charlie at Königstein in view of his what is now called trauma. He had also decided to ask permission to stay with Charlie as his friend and companion. Now when the situation was definite John made his demands, but, finding that I had become ill with dysentery during the night, put forward my name to take his place as Charlie's companion. This was an act of extreme selflessness since at that time salvation seemed to lie at Königstein rather than in the journey south, a journey which might well bring about the end of us all. The German Commandant needed no prompting and on his own initiative he agreed to keep Charlie and myself without communicating with higher authority. This was commendable and much more so than the recent action of the Colditz Commandant.

With a feeling of intense personal relief, and with great concern for the safety of the others, we waved them goodbye as their bus drove off towards the south. As it turned out, their journey ended without disaster. The Commandant, anxious to speed our recovery, moved us to a more comfortable room in the basement of his own quarters where we had paintings to look at and furniture to enjoy. Outside in the garden the Colonel's two boys played and laughed and reminded us of a life without war, without any of the cruelties and hardships we had endured. We were given food from the Commandant's own kitchen. With these benefits we both felt better. Charlie's tension disappeared and he regained his poise and sense of fun. The problem now was that his recovery was so great that we would lose our excuse for staying and the German Commandant would lose his excuse for keeping us. In the meantime we were making hay while the sun shone. The spring sunshine flooded into the Commandant's garden and I was free to wander around in it painting its views and its more intimate corners.

Our peaceful life was punctuated with visits from our friends with whom we were still at war, from Colonel Hesselmann and his Intelligence Officer, Major Sieber, who arrived with surreptitious presents of vermouth and cigars hidden in his attache case. For the time being Hesselmann, perhaps through a wish to maintain a correct relationship with us who were still his prisoners, retained a formal distance, but his Intelligence Officer, a slightly vulgar man whom we christened Porky, took full opportunity to unburden himself of his thoughts and feelings about the past. His love for German culture and German morality had led him into an acceptance of the Nazis, which had only been diminished by what had happened to the Jews. We soon realized that both visitors needed our help – Hesselmann because he was preparing himself for the ordeal of surrender to the Russians, whom he greatly feared and disliked, and Sieber because he was at the mercy of his mental conflicts about the past. Suddenly the tables had turned. We were the dominant ones and the Germans were looking to us for support.

We were desperate always to have good news. Until now we had been kept informed of how the war was going because we usually had a war correspondent or two among us and there were always crystal sets tucked away in the recesses of our camps. So we were kept in touch with how the war was going and there was never any doubt for most of the time that we would win. The great question was how soon; the sooner the better. Now when the end was excitingly close we suffered from a news blackout. There were plenty of rumours but no facts.

We also received visits from our allies – from General Bourret representing the French generals, of whom several hundred were imprisoned in the fortress. General Bourret described in detail the escape of General Giraud, who had collected material for a rope long enough to suspend a basket down the rock. With the help of the basket he had been lowered to safety below, where by careful planning a car had been waiting to drive him to the frontier. The generals were able to confirm for us our good opinion of Colonel Hesselmann, and they undertook to help us to do everything possible to protect the Germans when the Russians arrived. We were also called on by General Winkelman, the Dutch Commander-in-Chief, and his Chief of Staff, General Forst van Forst, who both impressed us with their spirit and their courage.

Himmler's expected telegram arrived some three or four days after our arrival. In it he ordered the Commandant to send us south immediately to join the others. This was an order which Colonel Hesselmann found difficult to disobey realizing, that if he did so he was putting his own life at risk. However, he was prepared to do so providing he could do it with a clear conscience on the grounds of our sickness. He knew that Charlie was better. The question now was whether my illness might be used as a justifiable reason for keeping us at Königstein. Porky came over to discuss the problem and it was agreed that the German camp doctor would be asked to examine me and report on my condition. As soon as Porky had gone, Charlie and I began to worry about the danger we were in. We decided to take no chances and, as an added incentive to my innards, we got down to cooking up some prunes and figs which were in our Red Cross parcel. When these were ready, I proceeded to swallow as many as I could stomach in the hope that they would start to stimulate the irrigation of my plumbing system. When the doctor arrived and began to prod my intestines, he might have been squashing a hot water bottle. Amazed by the liquid state of my insides, he went off to compile a report which would corroborate my evidence and which would justify the Commandant in disobeying the order to move us south. Charlie and I relaxed once more.

About a week later we heard the news that Admiral Doenitz had taken over the chaotic mess that Hitler left and was ready to ask for an armistice. We also heard rumours that Hitler was dead.

Then, some days after that, the Russians arrived. The evening before had been spent with the Hesselmanns in the cosy atmosphere of their candlelit sittingroom. The evening, which reminded us in so many ways of family life, with their sons appearing downstairs in dressing gowns after their bath, was punctuated by calls to the telephone. At one point we heard Colonel Hesselmann issuing orders to a local garrison which was under his command to surrender to the Russians. Some time during the evening he discussed the disposal of the Saxon Crown Jewels which were stored in twelve suitcases and were worth some £3,000,000. In his anxiety to prevent them falling into the hands of the Russians, he asked whether Charlie and I could take them home with us as a present to the British Royal Family. This we agreed to do, subject to our finding transport. The problem of the Dresden paintings which were also housed in the fortress seemed less easy, and as we examined the huge canvases standing on their ends against wooden partitions, we decided that the removal of these priceless works of art had to be the responsibility of qualified experts.

Then, towards the end of the evening, the door opened and a haggard and distraught looking officer came in, having left his motorbike at the foot of the stair outside. Our visitor, Baron von Friesen, confirmed what we already guessed, that the Russians were within five miles and would arrive next morning. He said they were burning and raiding and were out of hand. Having delivered his report, the Baron put his field glasses and map case on one side and sank exhausted into a chair. Charlie and I then went to our room to collect a small present of coffee for Frau Hesselmann as a token of our appreciation of her care and kindness to us. Colonel Hesselmann in his turn took off his small ceremonial sword and gave it to me as a token of his respect, and perhaps of his surrender, since he preferred to acknowledge the British rather than the Russians as masters of the field. This dagger is preserved at Bemersyde. The Colonel also gave me a key of the store of food which he wished to be protected from the Russians and distributed as and when the need arose.

Then the Colonel asked us to do our utmost to help the German women, of whom a hundred or more had gathered together for shelter in the fortress and for protection from Russian assault. Knowing of the French undertaking to help us in this matter, we indicated our resolve to do our utmost to safeguard the lives and bodies of the German women. Having made these undertakings and with mixed feelings about the morrow, we repaired to bed. This was to be the last night of our captivity.

10

Freedom

It was now April 1945. The war in Europe was coming to an end. I was liberated with my fellow Prominente Charlie Hopetoun by the Russians who had crossed the River Elbe below us in small boats. Their arrival and their animal behaviour distressed our German captors who looked to us for protection. Our sympathies were particularly with our Commandant, Oberst Hesselmann, and his family, who had shielded us from the clutches of Hitler and Himmler.

We watched the Russians from the ramparts as they advanced in small groups across the landscape – tiny dots darting from scene of havoc to scene of havoc, burning and looting as they went. Then a number of soldiers got into a boat and ferried themselves across the Elbe below us and from there, without any military formation and without haste, in motley groups proceeded up the hill to take over the castle which now had a white flag flying from the tower.

The castle became a turmoil. Russian soldiers, many of them drunk, were charging around without purpose other than to assuage their thirst for food, drink, property and possibly women. They were like naughty children, completely out of hand. The condition and behaviour of their officers was no better. During this senseless orgy the German soldiers, with Hesselmann at their head, were formed up on the terrace and marched off, according to rumour, to Siberia, while we were left surrounded by hysterical women clamouring to us for protection. Charlie and I, anxious to protect the dependants of our enemies in the face of the ferocity of our allies, helped some girls to hide and then went off like policemen on separate beats to protect other women from the Russians. Realizing that our peace-keeping role was in need of some support, I went off to see the French generals and summon their aid. The French did nothing, preferring to remain aside, merely watching the misfortunes of these unhappy women. I suppose they were within their rights. They had some reason because the SS had at one point taken one of the French generals and shot him in retribution for the escape of General Giraud from Königstein. So there was a bone of contention between the French and the Germans which was to trap the guiltless Hesselmann.

In April of 1947 I was to ask a question in the House of Lords in order to have Colonel Hesselmann's name removed from the list of War Criminals. Hesselmann, who had risked his life to save Charlie Hopetoun and myself from being moved as Hitler's hostages when we were ill in his camp at Königstein, had in his turn when he was sick from a duodenal ulcer been handed over by us to the French authorities to answer an accusation in which he was said to have handed over a French general to the Gestapo. My question was reported in the *Daily Telegraph*:

"EARL HAIG, son of the British Commander in Chief in the First World War, asked the Government why Oberst Martin Hesselmann was arrested at Stillen Friden on 13th February and what causes led to his death on 22nd March.

"He explained that Hesselmann was Commandant of a camp in which he (Lord Haig) was for some time a prisoner of war. He was treated very fairly and he formed a high opinion of Hesselmann as a man. Hesselmann was never told he would be arrested or why. He was placed in a cell in the winter without heat or light and his coat and scarf taken.

"THE LORD CHANCELLOR, VISCOUNT JOWITT, replied that when Hesselmann was arrested there was no suggestion that his health was bad. Four days later he complained of sickness and the German doctor advised that although there was nothing serious he should go to hospital. A French escort was expected to take him into the French Zone, and when they arrived the Commandant told them personally about Hesselmann's condition. Hesselmann later died from a duodenal ulcer.

"LORD JOWITT undertook to see that the questions which had been raised were brought to the notice of Lord Pakenham, Chancellor of the duchy of Lancaster, the Minister for the British Zone of Germany."

John Hope, brother of Charlie Hopetoun, also asked a question in the House of Commons, and as a result I heard later that Hesselmann's name had been cleared and that Frau Hesselmann had received her pension.

But let us return to Königstein where I found Charlie dealing patiently with some Russians who were trying to molest Frau Hesselmann and remove her watch. Charlie, who seemed very adept at handling these difficult people, (he treated them like naughty children humouring them rather than confronting them) made Frau Hesselmann take off her watch and give it to him for safe custody. Then, when the Russians' fury was turned on him, he let them take the watch, which they proceeded to smash on the ground and then hand back, broken, to Frau Hesselmann.

During this turmoil a German officer who had hidden from the Russians shot himself dead. The other officers and their men who had, as we thought, been taken away on barges bound for Siberia, returned some hours later without food, having had all their possessions taken from them by the Russians.

Meanwhile, Mittai, our Maori servant, to whom I entrusted

the store cupboard key, had himself been affected by the general tumult. After making advances to a German girl, and having been repulsed, he had taken refuge in a bottle of brandy. Having drunk this, he was suffering from a state of alcoholic remorse. Years of privation had brought his pent-up emotions to the boil and he was now crying. At this point the German soldiers, having returned and needing food for their independent journeys to their homes, came to me for the contents of the food store. I had given the key to Mittai, who was now in this emotional state. I asked him to give me the key, but he refused, since the key was for him a symbol of his power over the enemy who had caused him so much suffering. I tried to explain the purpose of the key, but it was no use trying to reason with him in the state he was in. I tried to force it from him. He seized me round the throat and began to throttle me. He was stronger than I and, in spite of my struggles, I felt myself weaken in his furious grasp. I thought he would kill me. Luckily some streak of sense in his nature took control and he relaxed his hold and gave up the key. I then hurried with the key to the store where I found some food and doled it out to the Germans.

The German soldiers departed along their various ways, making for home as best as they could. The Russians also left us. Charlie and I were now free to walk around at our will, and while we waited two weeks for some transport to take us westwards to the American lines we walked in the town below and in the surrounding countryside, which was fresh and green with blossom on the fruit trees. One day we had tea in a farmhouse, where we met a group of Polish girls. These girls looked and seemed gay in their summer frocks, but beneath their gaiety there were hidden tattoo marks from their years in Auschwitz. One of them, an artist called Janina Tollick, became a friend, whom I was able to introduce later to some Belgian friends who helped her through her period of rehabilitation.

Soon after our liberation we had decided to ask an American pilot in the fortress to try and get through on a bicycle to Chemnitz to ask for transport. Meanwhile we waited. Much of the time was spent in discussions with the Hesselmanns. The Commandant had now lost all his reserve of manner and became more open and free towards us. He showed us the 18th and 19th century records of the officers' training school which had been housed in the fortress. These records described the strict disciplines and training which the Junker officers had been ready to undergo, probably far stricter than anything their British contemporaries would have had to face. The curriculum had included duelling and fighting with razors. We talked about the past and future of Germany. During these discussions both the Hesselmanns kept repeating, "It will not be long before you will be fighting the Russians and then Germany and Britain will be on the same side." At this time there were long columns of pathetic-looking displaced Germans trudging back along the roads from the East. Individual Russians went up and down the columns harrying and marauding and molesting these wretched people who carried their few possessions in baskets or pushed them in prams or trolleys as they retreated westwards from the battlefields away from the rape and burning of their homes. Seeing one old lady lose her shoes and left to walk barefoot brought home the situation and gave us a feeling of compassion for the Germans, even though we had suffered so much at their hands.

One afternoon about two weeks after our liberation we were having coffee with the Hesselmanns when we heard a commotion outside. We looked out of the window and saw, first of all, some ambulances with Red Cross markings, some motor-bicyclists and then some armoured cars all drawn up in the courtyard, and behind them coming up the narrow winding road were tanks and anti-tank guns and a number of open camions. The castle became alive with a new invasion, this time a more orderly one, in the form of an American task force. The GIs had brought transport in response to the appeal sent through the American pilot. The task force had come ready to fight its way through and its commander was now keen to start back within two hours. Owing to the lack of warning, we had to leave without Mittai, who was lost in the town, but the transport had room for half the French generals and the Dutch generals as well as ourselves, and they promised to return for Mittai, the Hesselmanns and the rest of the French generals next day. The twelve suitcases of Saxon Crown Jewels had to be left, since life was more important than property. Happily they are now safely on view in a Dresden museum.

Charlie and I said goodbye to the Hesselmanns and got into the back of an armoured car. Behind us in a number of camions sat the French generals, five in a row, looking like black sambos because of the road dust which smothered them as they went along. Charlie and I could not see much from our armoured car, but I remember one policewoman from Russia on point duty directing traffic at a crossroads. Beside her was her loot in the form of a large grandfather clock.

After about two hours' drive we reached the American Divisional Headquarters at Chemnitz, where we were made welcome and comfortable. Our breakfast next morning was more than I could face – waffles and syrup followed by spam. After breakfast Charlie and I and the Dutch generals were taken by air to Brussels. During the flight I became ill with dysentery, which had been stirred up by the tensions and by the journey. We flew over Cologne, where I was relieved to see the cathedral still standing, although most of the city around it was flattened. At Brussels, due to my illness, Charlie was able to find places in a hospital plane belonging to 21st Army Group. As our plane took off, we left the Dutch generals sitting stranded on the tarmac. One of them, General Van Forst, had done his best to make a US pilot fly them home. He had explained that he was personal ADC to Queen Wilhelmina and wished to go to The Hague. "Where the hell's The Hague anyway?" had been the American's only response.

The hospital plane flew straight to England. Because we could not see out of the cabin I read the *Daily Mail* lying in my bunk. This was the first British paper I had read for about six years and I was amazed by the tone of its anti-German propaganda. Little did the British realize how utterly beaten the Germans were. After a while I got up and sat in the pilot's cabin during the plane's flight up the Thames low over the City of London.

We landed at Ampney Aerodrome, amidst the green fields of Gloucestershire. From there Charlie was sent to London for check-ups and dismissal. I was taken to the local hospital where I was left alone and frustrated on my first night at home. It was more than I could bear, to find myself pacing around inside four walls like a caged animal on the first night at home, a night to which I had so much been looking forward. My frustration was too great! I seized the telephone in the passage and rang my friend, John Cripps, who lived nearby. Luckily John was at home; he had himself recently been repatriated from a German POW camp and he knew exactly how I was feeling. He lost no time in driving to the hospital door through which I made my escape. As soon as I reached John's home I rang the hospital to tell them what I had done and where I was. They understood.

Next morning was Sunday. I awoke to hear the chime of the bells of the parish church, and I looked out to the chalk stream below the window and watched the brown trout rising to the mayfly. My sisters Doria and Rene came to fetch me. On the road to London we passed many beautiful young girls out walking with their lovers. As the reality of my return sank in, I began to weep.

It is difficult to explain my state of mind, except perhaps

to say that the whole system, physical and mental, was in a state of collapse as a result of three years of privation. On my return from Germany I still had severe attacks of dysentery, I weighed less than eight stone and my body was covered in boils. The doctors, after some persuasion, agreed that rest and fresh air, food and exercise were more desirable than being stuck in hospital, but I was asked to undergo a short treatment in the Officers' Nursing Home before going to the country for a period of rest and recuperation. Later, after several medical boards, I was categorized as C3 and discharged from the Army.

Readjustment to life after captivity was difficult. The affects of POW experiences had enabled me to find freedom through the inner freedom of dreams. Through them I had been taught some of the truths of my being in a world which lay far below the surface of the wartime lives of my relations and pre-war friends, many of whom found me withdrawn and changed.

We ourselves found the outside world changed. Relations and friends whom we had left behind had during the long six years adapted themselves in their own ways to total war. We had been through a different kind of experience and came out of prison so conditioned to the shackled life that we found it hard to adapt to the outside world. We were to some extent outcast from both the prison camp world and the world outside, so that, in times of despair, we lost the will to fight. This condition had in my case, and I am sure in the case of many others, been aggravated by an almost complete separation from women for six years at a most impressionable age, and at an age when most people are going through emotional development. Because of this emotional starvation, I did not feel as others felt who had lived a more normal life. I was living a full life at an intellectual level, so that I always had a book in my hand. But I was not able to live through the animal side of my nature, which because of its frustration came out into the open in the form of nightmares. Many of my dreams were to do with sexual fantasies and of amputations of various parts of my body. My depressions, which were almost worse than the depression I had suffered behind wire, seemed to come on for no particular reason. I was not happy among groups of people at parties, nor was I happy to be alone in the landscape, particularly when the sun shone brightly in summer.

There had been too much turmoil around us, caused by too many men living in a confined space. It was necessary to withdraw into ourselves for peace and quiet. Mostly there was a continual buzz of people talking, bargaining, selling or buying on the barter system, or in some way managing to interfere with our peace, our privacy and our powers to concentrate. Having been to a boarding school, I had been used to dormitories. Because so many young people were confined together there was an element of homosexual feelings at times. But I never came across any practising homosexuality. Apart from anything, the living spaces were so crowded that there would have been no privacy for that to happen.

Because we had been cut off from our friends and our families for so long we had lost touch with the realities of normal life. This made our friendships in the camps more important to us. Correspondence to and from home was very limited. Due to restrictions, we were only able to write the equivalent of an air mail letter every week or so. Letters from home were mainly limited to one's family. I had very few letters from anybody else. Other people were not encouraged to write. One of my old friends whose letters I greatly welcomed was Hugh Trevor-Roper and I always regard him as a true friend to have done that for me.

By the time I was taken prisoner the lives of my family at home had also become restricted and due to the restrictions of the censor their style was stilted. In contrast I remember a letter received when I was in Palestine in June 1940 from my sister Xandra (who was later to marry Hugh Trevor-Roper). This was more informative and fun. She wrote from Anglesey where she was staying with Aunt Violet:

"I came here for Whitsun just the day before the news of the German invasion of the Low Countries . . . Uncle Walter still thinks the war will end in June. I'm afraid he is very much mistaken and lives in a world of unreality. He is only bothering about what will happen after the war. He is afraid of revolution and capital levy. I say let us win this war, which is going to be a hard struggle. Things like capital levies are minor things compared with death and destruction which is what we shall probably all have to face. Uncle Walter has not laid up his Bentley in case the Germans should land here – 'Must have a fast car, me girl' – the tax on cars like that is simply prohibitive now. Aunt Violet is furious that he should waste money on this idea. I have knitted you a pair of khaki socks which I hope you will like and will be useful to you. Best love and do write a line when you have time. Xandra"

At the end of the war Xandra having married her first husband Johnnie Howard Johnston, who had won a DSO and DSC in the anti-U-Boat campaigns in the Atlantic was busily involved in cooking and nannying for her two young children. She was soon to move to Paris where Johnnie would be Naval Attaché and where she would study singing with Pierre Bernac.

My second sister Doria, who had been working in the Solex carburettor factory in the Marylebone Road, was living in London married to Andrew Scott who had commanded the Guards Brigade in North Africa and Italy and had won the DSO and bar. My third sister Rene, who had worked throughout the blitz in Bermondsey with the Red Cross, married Gavin Astor, an Oxford friend of mine, in August.

Uncle Walter Vivian had died in 1945 but Aunt Violet was

still living in Anglesey and able to provide for all of us a refuge in an atmosphere of love and security whenever we needed it. Our routine at Cestyll was of eating and sleeping bathing and sunbathing and lying in her beautiful rock garden. I was to enjoy that sheltered existence whenever a summer visit was possible. Aunt Violet had served as Lady in Waiting to Queen Alexandra. Like her mother, she was an expert needlewoman. I had always found her understanding, sympathetic and intelligent. She was beautiful and well dressed. Although her relationship with my mother was difficult she gave us all support.

I myself had changed. I had been made to think about who I was as a person and as an individual. I was less liable to be swept around by other people, so that I came over as a much more aware person. I had entered realms where there were conflicts but I was aware of the conflicts. So I was going into civilian life not taking things for granted. I found it difficult to come back to living life as one had lived it before. As new aspects of my personality began to emerge which I had not known before, I became aware of new pleasures and new experiences and in my self-awareness I became a fuller person able to stand on my own feet rather than be tossed around in the wake of others. At the same time, though I learnt to savour life fully, I learnt also to harbour my psychic energy rather than to disperse it in irrelevant distractions, and by committing it to art I was able to interpret nature in terms of rhythms which had vitality.

After my treatment in the Officers' Nursing Home I travelled to stay with Walter and Mollie Buccleuch at Drumlanrig, where, instead of being among a thousand other officer prisoners, I found myself in the Duke's private apartments, while the rest of the castle was occupied by a girls' school which had been evacuated from Edinburgh. My hostess, with her usual sensitivity, left me alone or kept me company according to my need and let me absorb in my own way the beauty of the setting and the works of art which filled the house. Walter took me with him on his journeys through the woods to mark the trees before felling by German POWs encamped on the estate. To see so many Germans working in the area made a strange impact on my mind, and I found I had an ambivalent attitude towards them. Although they had caused such havoc in the world and done me harm, my recent experiences of the behaviour of the Russian soldiers, and the help and kindness I had received at the hands of my last Commandant, had done something to remove the feeling of intense loathing which, as was only natural, I felt for the Germans on repatriation. I realized the seriousness of the plight in which the Germans now found themselves, how much their country and their cities were in ruins. Nevertheless, it took several years before I could revisit the country of which I had been so fond before the war, and I have never since been able to rid myself of an inner distrust of the German nation.

Hutchings, the butler, lent me a rod and sea-trout flies with which I cast for rainbow trout in Bridgeknowes Loch at the end of the park. I used the boat which I found in the boathouse below the beech trees and rowed quietly out through the reeds to where the large fish, left undisturbed throughout the war years, were feeding. Each evening I caught several trout which, with their pink flesh, made a welcome addition to our table. Thanks to the good food and healthy life, and to the efforts of my sister Doria, who poulticed my boils, my health improved.

In August I showed some of the POW paintings which I had brought back in the Scottish Gallery in Edinburgh in aid of Lady Haig's Poppy Factory and the Red Cross. The exhibition was visited by Her Majesty The Queen and the two Princesses.

I was also at the annual conference of the Women's Section of the British Legion, Scotland, which was attended by their Royal patron, the Queen.

At the end of the summer and on the advice of Raymond Mortimer, the art critic, I decided to apply for a place at the School of Art and Crafts, Camberwell. I was accepted by the Principal, William Johnstone, a fellow Borderer, after an interview in which he asked me, "Why do you want to come to a place like this?" And then, before I had time to reply, pointing at his own abstract of Scott's view painted near my home hung behind his desk, he went on to say, "You ought to be up there!" Knowing that my path would eventually take me home, I merely said that I wished to be taught how to paint so that I could embark on a career as a painter. I did not realize at the time the extent of the frustration from having to live south of the Borders that caused William's volcanic outburst.

My work at Camberwell did not change all that much. I had painted fairly regularly in POW camps the portraits of my fellow prisoners. Through reading books by André L'Hôte and others I had absorbed those same ideas of Turner and Cézanne which were followed by members of the Euston Road School who were teaching at Camberwell. My teachers were also at that time followers of Sickert who in most ways was the antithesis of Cézanne. Euston Road painters represented a reaction against the subjectivity of abstraction. Coldstream's ideas on the training of observation prevailed. They arose from a distrust of the easy charm of modern art. An attempt would be made to look without preconceptions – the looking being more important than the likeness. These views were to lead towards those of Anton Ehrenzweig in a book called *The Hidden Order of Art* in which he described the creative friction between inner and outer reality. The artist had to face chaos in his work before unconscious scanning brought about its integration. In his words, "The primary process is a precision instrument for creative scanning that is far superior to discursive reason and logic." Creative passages of paint based on close observation of nature were part of a heightened vision. Our privilege at Camberwell was to receive thought-provoking criticism about our work from four very good painters, Coldstream, Rogers, Pasmore and Gowing. Each spoke from his own personal viewpoint, though sharing a collective strictness about drawing of which Ingres would have approved. This strictness about verisimilitude did inhibit a number of students. Perhaps I had matured to a position of safety where I was able to give freedom to my fantasy by occasional distortions. We were encouraged to make renderings of masterpieces in the National Gallery, not by working in front of the paintings in the Gallery but back in the studio at Camberwell with the aid of a postcard photograph. I interpreted the Nativity by Piero Della Francesca in this way.

It was with Bill Coldstream's encouragement that I made a study of this great work. Though I tried to draw with precision the group of five angels and the Virgin at prayer and the Christ child, I left the other forms relatively vague. Looking at my work today makes me surprised by the lack of completion of those forms. There was another teacher, Tom Monnington, who did not let me get away with it. A year later, having painted a large nude over three weeks, I was told that the only passage of painting was round one ankle. The overall linear rhythms of the Nativity were understood without emphasizing the geometry which lay below them and the perception of a Mediterranean light was conveyed with truth and feeling. The exercise must have been worthwhile. It encouraged me to learn to handle a broad landscape with figures. By not niggling over details I was able to avoid losing the overall construction. Perhaps it encouraged me to paint simply and in a relaxed way to convey the feeling of that Holy scene better than if I had copied the original painting in the National Gallery.

In August, while staying with my sister Xandra at Bembridge, I met Dierdre Hart Davis who told me about a cottage available in her village of Sutton Petworth. I stopped off to see Rose Cottage on my way back to London, liked it and decided to buy. This provided an opportunity to paint the landscapes of West Sussex for the next three years. Happily in nearby South Harting lived my old friend Paul Maze who, during vacations from Camberwell, would provide, with his wife Jessie, warm companionship. I had known Paul since 1929. He had moved to this country after the First World War in which he had fought with gallantry as Liaison Officer between Army Headquarters and the front line. His unique experiences in the turmoils of French warfare are described in his book *A Frenchman in Khaki*. It so happened that on a visit to the 5th Army Headquarters in early 1918 my father had been able to pin a military medal on his gallant chest. Paul was a very romantic Frenchman in the best sense. He was no doubt lucky to survive the war. In earlier years he had met Corot and was a friend of French painters like Segonzac, Monet and Bonnard. Most particularly, he admired Vuillard whose work portrayed the intimacy of domestic life which was in strong contrast to the life of a wartime man of action. Settled on the borders of Sussex and Hampshire, Paul was in tune with nature and the seasons. In the course of time he abandoned working in oils, preferring to catch nature on the wing with very personal pastel interpretations of the domestic life of Jessie and of flowers. Living entirely in the country and working in the Monet tradition did not altogether satisfy him. He needed to portray life. So, very often he took off to paint at Goodwood and Newmarket, at Cowes or Henley. Above all his reputation is based on his portrayals of military ceremonial which he painted standing on the fringe of the Horse Guards near the throng of men and horses but sufficiently detached to be able to listen to the inner rhythms of his vision.

Paul had great humanity, a quality which is shared by Frenchmen working in their tradition of art. My close relationship with Paul began when I was starting to paint professionally and he was able to help me in all sorts of ways as a landscape painter and as a person. His work was full of life and reflected his enjoyment of the senses. This attitude was a change from all the inhibitions and deprevations which I had suffered as a POW and was a counterbalance to the austere teaching of the Euston Road painters who were my real mentors at this time. They were younger and more vigorous. They were single-minded in their attempts to find a way forward for young British artists. They were scrupulous in their methods of building masses and then building the image by careful measurement. Their methods were more plodding than Paul's in order to create the forms of nature in terms of classical space. Although Bill and Paul were not in disagreement, Paul had no wish to go beyond the immediacies of the natural scene which he interpreted in terms of colour modulations and classical rhythms. He was making indications in the wake of Cézanne's watercolours rather than using his pastels in the tradition of Degas to convey a stronger and more complete image, as the Euston Road painters were aiming to do.

I responded to the happy atmosphere in the School, looked forward to the No 36 bus journey each day anxious to get out my palette and down to work as quick as possible. I was as keen as any student to respond to the variety of teachers each making his own contribution of thought to help me grow. My work continued to grow as it had grown in the prison camps. They were like gardeners regularly giving me great dollops of water from their watering cans. So through their vision the frozen purple flesh of the models, due to the inadequate heating, was transformed. Apart from Richard Rees, I made few close contacts with my fellow students, many of whom were of a younger age. I do not know what impression I made on them but some of them may have been quietly intrigued. According to Louise Reid (née Young): "There was a cross little man in the office who was never very helpful, but every now and then he would come puffing up the stairs and along the corridor into our silent painting room and approached a particular student saying, 'Telephone for you, sir'. We all wondered why he should get such special treatment; then we found out it was Earl Haig's son." What the telephone calls were about I cannot remember, but for my part any interruptions in my painting time were very unwelcome.

According to Elspeth Buchanan I needed feeding up. "The Euston Road Group had much the same point of view as the Edinburgh College of Art. Abstract art was not encouraged and one developed realism. I remember few students but one that remains in my mind was Earl Haig (I suppose because he was Scottish). At every model rest time he had to go and have a glass of milk. He had just returned from a German prisoner of war camp and was in poor health."

Richard Rees was a friend of George Orwell and editor of Simone Weil's letters. Although he was a beginner at painting he became very good, thanks to application. A self-torturer by nature he twisted his body into contortions of agony as he measured the proportions of the model before him. He and I worked all day and we went home separately to our bedsitting rooms at night dead tired, too tired for much social life. Quite often I had quiet evenings with Laurence Gowing and Julia Strachey in Wellington Square and with Victor and Wendy Pasmore at Hammersmith. By the summer of 1947 I began to go to dances. I went to Ascot races, during which I had the honour of being invited to the ball at Windsor Castle, a place of some meaning for me, since it was at Windsor during Ascot Week that my father had met my mother and become engaged. I was received with warmth by the King, whom I had not met since the time of his Coronation in 1937, when I had been his Page of Honour. At the ball I saw Princess Marina, Duchess of Kent, with whom

I felt a close affinity, perhaps because there was a certain isolation in her situation as a foreign war widow in Britain, and I also shared her feeling for painting. She herself was an amateur painter of great talent, and her father before her had been a painter also. She came over to see me some days later at my cottage in Sussex looking beautiful in a gorgeous summer dress and a carnation in the buttonhole of her camel-hair overcoat. Beneath the shyness of her manner there lay a warmth and dynamism, an understanding of people and of life which was stimulating.

I shall always be grateful for the inspiration Princess Marina gave to me and for her friendship. It was my regret that I did not do more to encourage her to practise the art of painting for which she had so much talent. When the Princess died this country lost a very special personality. She brought to her public duties the qualities which can only be acquired through suffering and through a meaningful private life. Her father was a painter, and she was brought up in considerable poverty in Paris. She had very much the make-up of the artist and her work was full of insight into character. To know her and to be with her was to share things which only artists have in common.

Lawrence Gowing had a strong influence on my work in Sussex. He had a wide knowledge of painters of the past and a professional approach to the practicalities of landscaping. His preparations for the field, his selection of equipment and subject matter would have earned him promotion in the army. The places where our painting took place became trodden like battlefields after days of stamping about in the grass and nettles.

In August 1946 I left him behind at Rose Cottage in order to join Paul Maze at the Moulin in France. There I received several letters from Lawrence which were heartfelt in their sincerety about painting and the need to share his feelings:

"The 24 x 18 I put paid to the day before yesterday and left my pitch for the last time, now a trodden mud patch, bare, smeared and oozing, like the place where a cow has died. But I left it half weeping, I was sorry to see the last of it, oak and ash tangled with burdock and cow parsley, a sublime spot and I've been very happy in it. I wonder how many mornings painting I had on that picture? Counting up in the diary I've been keeping I make it 8 or 9 visits, averaging 1½ hours I suppose. How does this compare with your practice?"

He wrote about the difficulties in keeping to a routine, the difficulties in finding a subject, and the problem of actually doing the job. Lawrence was a super professional and he hoped perhaps a little forlornly that all that he wrote would be absorbed by me. Most of it was, but at that time I was still finding my way in life as well as painting, so I evaded some of the disciplines which Lawrence tried to instil. Later in life I came to regret that I had not taken more advantage of what Lawrence had to offer:

"What do you think one's looking for when one's wandering round in search of a subject? It's quite a mystery to me. There are grades of painters just as there are grades among the religions. The common or garden inferior kind of devotee needs a church or chapel of a specific variety, a special service, a priest – the saint, however, can get his ecstasy anywhere, climbing a mountain or emptying a dustbin – anywhere. There's a kind of painter who can get his picture anywhere, or do you think that untrue? I've always thought the story about Corot and Courbet going painting together – Corot manoeuvring about murmuring endlessly about 'masses' and 'tone values' while Courbet sat straight down to work saying he always took things as they came. I've always thought it most suspicious. Courbet, bearing in mind his character, had probably rehearsed the act elaborately the day before and spied out the land. The whole thing's a mystery.

Often I begin by feeling I've been hunting for something I don't really need and end by concluding sadly that all the time I've only been pretending to have found it. (The first difficulty of course is one's tendency to set out to paint subjects that look like pictures instead of things one likes the look of)."

About his methods of composition Lawrence wrote:

"I've always been a very systematic painter. I learnt to paint (as an adult, that is to say I relearned) by the method Bill Coldstream used to teach (I don't know if he does still) called the 'pudding method' by which you make a pudding in the middle of the canvas of the right colour and tone and then cut slices off it until it's the right size and shape. At one time this method had I think great advantages for me but I now find I have very largely abandoned it. I think because I feel the need to think to some extent in line from the word go. In fact I find I'm beginning to believe (what I believed as a boy but should have regarded as the rankest heresy a few years or even a few months ago) that if one isn't making patterns one isn't making anything. The realistic painter trusts the patterns which design themselves, or trusts his unconscious or trusts his medium whatever you call it. But I think I have tended to translate this (I hope not when teaching) into a puritanical distrust of any deliberation any design at all."

Lawrence regarded my stay with Paul with some distrust:

"There was a hint in your letter, though, that you feel like subscribing to the doctrine that one should paint naturally, just like a bird sings, or it's no good at all. I feel quite sure that this is untrue. There are a few lucky, lyrical painters who've always played with paint and always will. Victor I imagine is one of them. But that is not the only kind of painting nor even always the best. One decides on one's premises, the hypothesis, the problem one's going to work at by a deep irrational process that one may as well call inspiration as anything else. And that problem like an itch is always there. But to carry it on to it's conclusion, solve it visibly and triumphantly, that's another matter. I certainly think that moral qualities, like determination, courage and integrity and intellectual ones are indespensable. One does, in fact, very often have to flog oneself to work and strangely enough that is sometimes when one paints best. One has to recognize it; there is certain resistance in one to producing anything, just as one resists being analysed, for instance. It is a question of telling a new truth which only one's own self knows and often the desire to tell it is only a tiny bit stronger than the desire not to give one's self away."

11

Return to Scotland

In 1948 Lawrence moved north as head of the School of Art at Newcastle just after I returned north. He came over the border several times and carried on communicating to me his strong love of landscape painting, though for him the Borders could never compare with his beloved Sussex.

Towards the end of 1947 my home at Bemersyde, which had been occupied by the Women's Land Army during the latter part of the war, became vacant and I moved in. Together with William Eastway, a former Sergeant in the Greys, Ted Ruffman, my factor, and with the guidance of the land agent, Colonel Guy German, who had been at Colditz, we were able to spend the winter working on improvements to the estate, which had been neglected during the war years. I reassembled my father's museum and opened the Peel Tower to the public. Rose Cottage in Sutton, bought after the war for the sake of countryside peace and as a place for landscape painting, was now redundant and put up for sale. Sadly I parted from a cottage which had helped me to adopt a painter's way of life and which had given me the privilege of walks in the unspoilt landscape of West Sussex. Equally sadly, I had to say goodbye to a much simpler way of life.

Bemersyde House had been badly let down due to lack of heating and bad maintenance during the war. Dry rot was discovered in the newer part of the building. My sister Xandra helped over the decoration and to enable me to pay for the costs I held a sale of surplus furniture.

I moved to Scotland with some reluctance knowing that my painting would have to take its place along with other responsibilities. So far my work had benefited from the atmosphere of camps and art school and from contacts with a variety of artists. Now I found myself in an environment which was in some ways hostile to the creative spirit. My various responsibilities made inroads into my painter's routine. About that time the Very Reverend Dr Charles Warr, Dean of the Thistle, opening my exhibition in the Scottish Gallery in Edinburgh, appealed that I might be allowed to devote my time to my new-found art of painting and be left free from the public commitments that my inherited title thrust upon me. "This northern country," according to Dr Warr, "was not so fortunate in having many fine artists. When one was discovered therefore, he should be left to devote his time to fuller expression." This appeal made some impact upon the minds of people who worked for Scottish charities and perhaps as a result some of them who felt eager to invite me to join them in their work refrained from doing so. His words also helped my own conscience and I was relieved to think that this great churchman who had himself written books and been wounded as a combatant in the First World War should think my work to be of sufficient merit to justify my refusing to take on too many duties. However, my life would lead me to many interesting and worthwhile voluntary jobs in the Legion, the National Galleries of Scotland and the Scottish Arts Council. To say to me "all you must do is paint" was to oversimplify the issue.

My life became complicated and at times I was torn in several directions at once, having to go off to Edinburgh for a meeting when the light for landscape painting was good. Many things attracted me. On good days when the light was strong and northern and swift-moving it transformed the landscape into interesting silhouettes and edges. I enjoyed the marks of a field where an implement had divided the wildness of nature from the smoothness of land worked by a tractor. At that time combines were rare and at harvest time the corn sheaves were gathered into stooks. All these facets of the landscape awoke in me some sort of spiritual and sensual response and drove me to want to draw. Sometimes, when drawing a subject, sketching from various points helped me to see its movements and also to discover what lay beyond. I started to move back and forwards with my camp stool. In this stage of immediate sensations and impulses my sketches had a spontaneity and vitality lacking in my later studio work. In sketching I found I did better if I left my oils behind and only took pencils, paper and a few watercolours. Nature was too complex for me to try and combine the sketching and painting stages together. In this country of changing light and weather I found it impossible to complete an oil painting out of doors.

Life assumed some of its prewar ease. Parties and horses took their place against the eternal background of Bemersyde and its garden of which Geordie Wilson, the gardener, though with a limp caused by a tree which had fallen on his leg while he was sawing, was still custodian. Friends came and went. Patrick Crosse came back from Switzerland where he had been recovering from the effects of tuberculosis contracted whilst a prisoner at Hadamar. He was soon to find happiness, alas short-lived, with the journalist Jenny Nicholson who was to die at a tragically early age. He himself was to die prematurely twenty years later.

On New Year's day Lawrence wrote from Wellington Square: "I've got the Newcastle job and have been ex-changing cordial letters with Lord Eustace Percy, whom I liked very much. I nearly didn't get it, and you'd be amused to hear that it was because they thought I'd obviously be no good at organization." This assumption, I could have told Lord Eustace, was far from correct from my knowledge of Lawrence's habits and qualities. Indeed too much of his time and energy were given to administration. Richard Rees became a regular visitor and with him I painted landscapes. I badly needed contact with someone else working on Euston Road lines.

For Christmas 1947 we had a family party which included Doria and Andrew and their son Douglas and daughter Henrietta and Aunt Violet. Xandra came over from her house in Melrose with her husband Johnnie Howard Johnston and their children James and Xenia. I had been lucky to find a splendid girl who came temporarily as parlourmaid and model, so Xandra and I were able to paint her in the studio. My painting of her was later bought by the Arts Council.

Victor and Wendy Pasmore arrived to stay in 1948, the first of several visits. Victor was still making drawings from the landscape, but his mind had moved on from the teachings of the Euston Road. His work had become more abstract in keeping with theories of basic form and of the Bauhaus and of Paul Klee in particular. His spiral motifs stemmed from his studies of the book *Growth and Form* by D'Arcy Thompson.

On my walls hangs a naturalistic landscape designed on geometric principles painted by Victor in Blackheath in 1947. Beside them are two abstracts painted in 1948 which are influenced by Paul Klee. This progression shocked many people, who regretted the switch from Whistlerian paint to the use of compass, newspaper and scissors. During his visit Victor and I went to the National Gallery in Edinburgh and on the way home in the train Victor made analytical drawings of the geometrical structure of some of the paintings. I particularly remember his analysis of Rembrandt's Hendrijke Stoffels. I also remember vividly our visit to the Buccleuchs at Bowhill when we stopped to enjoy the view of the Yarrow from the bridge. Victor remembered the ballad "The Dowey Dens of Yarrow" and his eyes lit with intensity as he contemplated the view. We also went over to visit the McEwens at Marchmont and the Ellesmeres at Mertoun to see their collections of paintings.

1947 was the beginning of the Edinburgh Festival, founded by Sir John Falconer, the Christies of Glyndebourne and Rudolf Bing, and which was to provide an annual feast of music over the years. Xandra brought, among others of her friends, Yehudi and Diana Menuhin and Pierre Bernac to Bemersyde. Another distinguished visitor was the elderly Sir Edward Marsh, whom I had to use as a cattleman after a young bull had escaped on to the lawn just as we were leaving fully dressed in dinner jackets for the opening concert. I positioned Eddie as a stop on the drive while Hugh Trevor-Roper and I advanced behind the animal which preceded us safely through the gate.

Robert Blake came up to edit my father's diaries and papers which were published in 1953. Although Lord Trenchard was against publication, my family and I decided in favour. My sister Doria put the position to me very clearly in a letter written in 1949:

"I cannot tell you how grateful I am to you for showing me the extracts from the Diary. You couldn't imagine how much pleasure they have given me. I have read them fascinated and enthralled. I have been transported back and it has been like spending evenings talking again with Daddy. It is extraordinary how strongly and vividly you recapture him, but I fear I am no person to judge as I have perhaps an exaggerated feeling for him. Mummy was so difficult, Xandra never there and you and Rene so young while he was alive. Since then no one has ever seemed to get a glimmering of an appreciation for either his character or his achievements. Consequently I have preserved my own picture and realised with him that fundamentally what the world says is of no account as long as in your heart you know you have done what your conscience convinced you was best or right. I would very much like somebody quite unbiassed and ignorant to read these extracts. Would they get a valid idea of a man and would they follow the strategy coherently? I can't tell. I suppose there are many reasons to publish this book: 1. To exonerate Daddy as a general; 2. To dispel this idea of him as a man, that he was stupid, obstinate, unimaginative, ruthless, lacking in humour and humanity but honest, in fact the lowest form of Colonel Blimp; 3. Practical purposes are rather ruled out. There has been a bigger war since when people said we mustn't make the same stupid mistakes as last time (nine times out of ten referring to Daddy and Passchendaele); 4. It's a historical document; 5. To make money. The first two are the ones that matter, 4 would follow and 5 of no importance. It is infuriating to think that Douglas, [her son] as a history specialist and then Army candidate was told to read Liddell Hart as his Bible for the 14/18 war! Is it too personal to be a military document? I agree there is the official history for that but it is so long. I don't suppose 1% of the population of the British Isles even has read it. I certainly have not. Is any one interested? Is it neither new enough nor old enough history? Will it in fact do any more good than Duff's book and it has the bigger disadvantage of being post 39/45 war. Certainly it can't do harm and might do good, don't you think? Or will it just cause a lot of forgotten mud to be dug up and kicked around. Personally I think there is so much there where it doesn't belong that at the end the central figure would be as it should be, clean."

I am thankful now that we took the decision that we did. The edited parts of the testimony are, there published for historians to read as my father would have wished. As a result many of them, led by John Terraine, have been able to study the evidence and come to a fair assessment. The publication was given a mixed reception at the time and unfortunately, due to some of the criticisms of Foch being highlighted in French papers, the reception there was bad. The many tributes to Foch in the book were of course left out by the press. This was sad because the French generals have always had a great admiration for my father, as he had for them.

After Christmas 1948 at Drumlanrig I went to stay with Derek Hill near Florence in the Villino lent to him by Bernard Berenson. On several occasions we were asked to I Tatti, where Berenson presided at the head of the table in a state of eminence surrounded by his court, and listened to him pronouncing with clarity and lucidity and not without feeling on painting. On the first occasion he had announced during a lull in the conversation that he had heard from Hugh Trevor-Roper that no time would be wasted in my company and so he had been waiting impatiently for my arrival as if I was a Messiah. His barbed words, intended to goad me into talking, had the opposite effect and reduced me to tongue-tied silence. He was a great expert but his appreciation of modern art was limited; only Degas who carried on the strict classical traditions of the Renaissance found favour. By eliminating the freer expressionistic aspects of modern art he was depriving himself of work which explored the inner vision. Among the painters who failed to find favour was Morandi, whom Derek and I visited one day at Bologna. We found the great painter and his two sisters at home in a small studio flat in a modern apartment block. The sisters shared a room with a Madonna hanging above their beds. Perhaps the very ordinariness of the surroundings helped Morandi to be transported into a metaphysical state of mind, as he meditated in front of his tin boxes with their painted sides. He gave Derek a small lyrical study of white flowers, which Berenson examined with little approval on our return.

Morandi's way of life seemed to me simple, and he was shocked by the high prices which his dealers were able to ask for his work. His life and work had a delicacy to which the attitudes of our materialistic society were alien. He reduced the sunlight in his studio by means of a gauze screen which he attached to his windows, and by this means a diffuse light was filtered on to the objects of his still life, which had been specially selected or painted to give a pleasing relationship of shape, tone and colour, so that they became the jumping-off point for a visual and spiritual experience. He spent many hours contemplating the objects of the still life, until they began to dance in his mind. When he had established mentally the approximate position of colour against colour, surface against surface, he began to paint. The actual painting took only a short time, perhaps two hours, but during that time he was able to establish the exact rhythms of the dance. His technique was to use only a few colours put on directly and cleanly. The greys and whites of his bowls and boxes were interpreted in terms of warm and cool greys, which he made up with white, cobalt green and burnt sienna and a touch of black. He made a few accents with cobalt violet or lemon yellow, cobalt blue or Venetian red. With these colours the verticals of his boxes were elongated or reduced according to the dictates of his imagination. With his sensitive brush strokes the marble jars and tin boxes were caressed into a life of their own. The dance began. He also selected landscapes from which he chose certain sequences of form, of horizontal skylines and roofs against vertical buildings and trees which he saw against the soft light of evening or early morning, when certain relationships of tone and colour were found to trigger off his response.

In 1949 I had two exhibitions. My first London exhibition

was at the Redfern Gallery thanks to the invitation from their Director, Rex Nan Kivell. Amongst my letters was one from Eddie Marsh: "I must congratulate you most warmly on the pictures. There's a peculiar grace and tenderness in your vision of things which make each one a pleasure to look at. I liked particularly the two large 'Gala Waters' and how good the Gillie is. You ought to do more portraits."

The second exhibition was at the Scottish Gallery in Edinburgh during the Festival. The Queen came and bought a landscape of the Borders. Afterwards Derek Hill wrote:

"Dawyck seriously your exhibition showed more promise than any first show I have ever seen. It was far above most exhibitions of old hands as you yourself know and you must go at it, hard." One of the paintings at that time was titled 'The Mailbag Sewer', a subject which evolved out of a series of visits which I made to HM Prisons at the invitation of Lord Templewood, who asked me to advise on art therapy for delinquents. I visited a number of different kinds of prisons and in nearly all of them I found men following a dull routine without meaningful occupations.

I had been reading Oscar Wilde's description of his imprisonment in *De Profundis* and my thoughts had kept focusing on Penal Reform. I had met during the summer William Douglas Home who looked grey and haggard after a term of imprisonment imposed on him for refusing to obey an order to attack a French village with his platoon, an order which he had considered to be inhumane. William had given some graphic descriptions of conditions in civilian gaols and I began to think out ways and means of reducing the harmful effects of prison sentences on men and women who under the present scheme seemed to turn only too easily into recidivists rather than emerge from their first sentence as improved persons and as persons deterred from the path of crime.

It seemed to me from my experiences as a POW that one of the possible ways by which prisoners might be helped towards an improved state of mind and heart lay in the sphere of art therapy. With this in mind and with the aid of some lessons which I learnt as a result of a tour of some prisons I was able to compile a report for Lord Templewood which may have had a small impact on the efforts which the Howard League for Penal Reform were making to improve conditions in the prisons. Perhaps my efforts also contributed in a small way to the improvement of facilities for prisoners so that their creative energies were not stultified by work in the mailbag sewing room. My visits to prison had enabled me to think of other people who were suffering hardship and, by diverting my thoughts on to the problems of finding alternative tasks for civilian prisoners, I had been able to relieve my mind of some of the frustration I felt as a result of my experience in POW camps. In order not to confine my activities to investigation and to theories I tried my hand at lecturing. I borrowed a set of slides of some of my favourite paintings from the Victoria and Albert Museum to illustrate some talks to the inmates of Wormwood Scrubs.

In 1948 I had written an article in *The Times* to stress the need for art therapy to which my old headmaster, J.F. Roxburgh, had responded:

"Dear Dawyck,
    I really must congratulate you on your letter in *The Times*. The thought that a man may be shut up, perhaps for years, and not allowed to produce anything from his mind or make anything with his hands is frightful. Your letter must do good in pointing out what I suppose most of us have known but never fully realised.
All best wishes."

In November 1949 Victor wrote from Blackheath:

"My dear Dawyck,
    I was very glad to hear from you although you seem

depressed, what can I say? We are not professional painters today in the same sense as Raphael or Rubens. The foundations of our art are within us and in the long gaps between moments of inspiration we suffer from boredom and restlessness. The great modern painters have all had to fight this, Cézanne, Degas, Gauguin, Van Gogh. It is necessary to set oneself a problem to solve, a goal to reach which unites our work and to which the subjective mind can cling.

"I agree with your sentiments about craftsmanship, it is that which gives full and proper expression to the form. But we must beware of those crocodile tears about machinery. It is not the machine which is the cause of poor craftsmanship, but the stupidity of those who do not know how to use the machine. Man has always used machinery to assist him in his art, but there are some who expect the twenty-five-ton electric engine to produce the same kind of thing as the potter's wheel. New machinery must inevitably produce new forms of art proper to this machinery. The photographs are first rate. Your work increases from strength to strength and moreover embodies a distinctly personal aesthetic. Don't listen to those mischief makers who, in the press, have been trying to equate your work with mine.

I hope you are well. Wendy joins me with all good wishes.

Yours ever

Victor"

Victor remained a good friend, mentor and critic until his death nearly fifty years later. He was quiet and deeply contemplative, though he enjoyed company and understood people. He took the trouble to visit my occasional London exhibitions and sometimes altered the hanging.

I was to see Lawrence less and less after he left Newcastle and eventually became head of the Slade. He had invited Victor to be head of the Painting School at Newcastle, and had been willing to encourage the teaching of the modern theories of basic form. He himself continued to follow the

Euston Road approach to drawing and painting which involved the flexible building up of masses and a willingness to change the form according to the slow dictates of observation and correction. He was at his best in small oil landscapes painted on boards in the lid of his paint box. Soon after he reached Newcastle he parted from Julia Strachey and married the daughter of a Northumbrian farmer. I attended the wedding in a small country church. Bill Coldstream was best man. After the wedding we all had lunch in a setting which might well have been painted by Courbet. The marriage did not last long and then Laurence returned to Julia and finally married her.

In September I spent a short holiday at Birkhall and then with my old brother officer Alwyne Farquharson and his wife Francie at Invercauld. Then in October 1949 I was asked by Charles Lambe, Captain of HMS *Vengeance*, to go with him on a cruise to the Cape Verde Islands where he and I would paint the landscape. I joined him at Gibraltar and luckily I arrived two days early as it gave me time to realize that living in an aircraft carrier would be too claustrophobic. With Charles's understanding I changed the plan and instead spent the rest of the holiday in Madrid with his wife, Peter, who in Charles's words "was a unique companion. One must cut adrift all ties to normal conventional life and you find she leads you off into some quite unexpected fairyland which has been at one's elbow all the time. It is a great gift and I'm sure nobody would appreciate it more than you."

We spent much of the time in the Prado and saw one bull-fight during which I made a number of drawings which I used in several paintings the following winter.

In November I was made Chief of the Haig family. The Scotsman recorded:

"The ancient banner of the Haigs, whose motto is 'Tyde what may,' will again float over the tower of Bemersyde, near St

Boswells, which has been for centuries associated with that famous Scottish family. The Lord Lyon King of Arms has granted to the 2nd Earl Haig, Lord Haig of Bemersyde and 30th Laird, rematriculation of the arms of Haig of Bemersyde, and the right to style himself Chief of the Name of Haig.

"Giving judgement at the Autumn Head Court, the Lord Lyon (Sir Thomas Innes of Learney, KCVO) said that the 2nd Earl was the son and heir of the Field Marshal, for whom part of Bemersyde was bought in 1920 as a national recognition of his services. The first Earl himself acquired the house of Bemersyde from Arthur B. Haig, 28th Laird.

"The Field Marshal recorded a shield in 1902 indicating his genealogical position in the family, but after 1920 he came to consider that he should be Chief of the Haigs.

The Chain of Inheritance

In Lyon Court, the Lord Lyon pointed out, every petitioner must prove his case and his right to the arms he claimed, and no one but the person found entitled could be revested in the undifferenced arms. The armorial history of Bemersyde emphasised the well-known medieval tendency to regard the inheritor of the family estate as the Chief, whether he was heir male, heir of line, or genealogically a cadet.

"Lyon Register showed numerous examples of cadets inheriting an ancestral estate by some devolution or tailzie getting the undifferenced arms as Chief."

In 1920 a group of subscribers had bought Bemersyde from the 28th Laird, Arthur Balfour Haig, and had presented it to his close cousin my father.

"The question was whether the transaction of 1920 between the 28th Laird and the Field Marshal, and creation of the dignities, constituted an 'inheriting' or a mere sale. The Lord Lyon did not think the parties themselves were clear about this, and he felt that, on the face of the deed, he could not treat the transaction of 1920 as alone sufficient. It would open the door to any cadet purchasing an ancestral estate and setting up a claim to the chiefship, even where this had not been the vendor's intention. Fortunately Nigel Haig, son and heir of the 28th Laird, had now conveyed to the present Earl the chiefly and armorial rights which his father, the 28th laird, had right under the entail of 1878 thus perfecting the transaction of 1920. Earl Haig thus became entitled to the undifferenced chiefly arms and to be Chief of the Name Haig."

At that time I was encouraged by George Todd, then Colonel of the Regiment, to be Chairman of the Royal Scots Greys Association, Edinburgh Branch. The membership included a number of veterans from the First World War and even the Boer War. I was later succeeded after thirteen years by Aidan Sprot whom I had known as childhood neighbours, at Stowe, and in the Regiment.

That autumn I began to participate in the affairs of the British Legion. Although I resisted major commitments I became President of the Border Area. Eventually this was to lead to major commitments including the National Chairmanship of the Legion in Scotland and later to the Presidency. I was also at that time President of Lady Haig's Poppy Factory, which my mother had founded in 1926 in Edinburgh.

I was also helping with the setting up of the Studios and Workshops Foundation which led to the Scottish Craft Centre of which I became President and John Noble of Ardkinglas became Chairman. I also became an Elder of Mertoun Church.

I continued to absorb the Border landscape and to interpret it in terms of abstract colour and form. The Borders to my mind are more interesting than the Highlands because there is more detail. One of the difficulties these days is to find nature which is not too much spoilt by forestation or farming or modern roads. The roads around Selkirk have been straightened, causing the loss of many subjects. I think that nature has been altered quite considerably. Farmers plough up their arable land immediately after harvest so that we do not have those lovely stubble fields in late October. In my early days there were stooks to draw. Bringing civilization to the Borders has been to the detriment of the landscape painter. There is plenty of Sir Walter Scott in the atmosphere of the Borders but my inspiration never came from literature. I simply look at nature in the footsteps of Turner. When Turner came, I don't think he was particularly inspired by the ballads and poems of Sir Walter, which he was required to illustrate in the minstrelsy of the Scottish Borders. I do not think the ballads particularly affected what Turner did. He was simply recording the landscape in wonderful little studies and drawings which he used for making his illustrations when he got home. There is a difference between the work of the artist and of the literary person.

The purpose of this book has been to explain how I found some scraps of paper and a pencil and began to draw my fellow prisoners, of how I managed to pass the time in relative solitude. Thanks to advice from others and from books, my work had improved. I had been encouraged by Humphrey Guinness's description of his friend, who having been captured during the First World War, had bounced a tennis ball endlessly against a wall with a stick and who had come home to become a Wimbledon player. I had the good fortune to come home with an enhanced talent which might take me somewhere along the road as an artist.

During that time I had also met people with different experiences and outlook from my own and been able to think out my own identity. I was thus able to prepare myself for the postwar world in which I would play a part quite different from the one which I would have played had the war not happened. Ironically, out of the evil that Hitler wrought upon my life there came some good.

Index